For my friends
Bill & Esther
with affection

Jerry

8/29/17

Bill: thanks for your help
with this book.

Jerry Lindenstraus

An Incredible Journey

From East Prussia, via Shanghai and Colombia to New York
A Jewish Family History
1929 to 2017

Hartung-Gorre Publishing House,
Konstanz, Germany

Front cover: Jerry on the ship to Shanghai, back cover: Jerry in New York 1999

© 2017 y Jerry Lindenstraus
All rights reserved
1ˢᵗ Edition 2017
Hartung-Gorre Publishing House, Konstanz, Germany
ISBN 978-3-86628-596-5

I dedicate this book to my son Leslie, because he agreed to travel with me to Shanghai, Bogota, and my birthplace Gumbinnen, otherwise this book would never have been written. Now he knows my background, and he can answer any questions his children and future grandchildren may have.

Many American friends asked me about my past when they heard my German accent, and when I told my story they would say, "write a book!" so finally I did. I wish I could thank many people for helping me to write it, but sadly they have all died, including my wife Erica. She encouraged me to keep writing, and she read, reread and corrected every page. Without her, I would not have finished the book.

Erhard Roy Wiehn, Sociology Professor at the University in Konstanz Germany is the publisher and editor of my book in German. My wife Erica and I visited him in Konstanz, a beautiful city on the lake, for a weekend, where he agreed to publish my book

Contents

PREFACE

My book was written in English and was translated to German and published in Germany in 1999. A lot has happened between 1999 and 2017, many good things, but also tragic ones. Most importantly—my wife Erica passed away suddenly on November 28, 2010; it was a tremendous shock to me and my son Leslie and his family. It was completely unexpected; we had plans to go out to dinner that night. I will never forget her; she guided me, gave me valuable suggestions, and kept me sane. I was blessed with two extraordinary grandchildren who kept me going during that tough time. Jessica was born October 29, 1999, and Aaron was born December 20, 2001. Since their births I have spent nearly every weekend babysitting. As they grow older I visit them, or we go out for dinner or to a movie. I was proud to be a part of their bat and bar mitzvahs. I moved from Washington Heights to the Upper East Side after Erica's death, starting a new life—living alone, which I enjoy. My beautiful apartment is conveniently located near movie houses, many stores, and public transportation. Most importantly, however, I live four blocks from my kids and grandchildren.

My export business called Lindeco International Corp. flourished, but I began to see changes: competition from China and India, and also from the Internet. Over the past 15 years, some of my good business friends passed away. The younger generation took over and I had no rapport with them. So I decided to sell. The company still exists in Miami, run by my friend Enrique Escobar.

An important new person came into my life a year after Erica's death, a woman named Margie. She is a wonderful person, a great companion. Our social life is an ongoing pleasure.

Sadly, this year brought with it more great losses: first, my best friend Gary Kirschner, whom I had originally met while living in Shanghai, passed away. We met over 70 years ago. Then Ernie Michel, my idol, a man I looked up to, also passed away.

I am a very lucky man, 88 years of age and still playing tennis, enjoying the 92nd Street Y, and my life with Margie. My wartime experiences have led me to lecture about my life in Shanghai and elsewhere, including Berlin.

Above all, and now more than ever, my family brings me joy: my son Leslie and his wife Michelle are very supportive and loving, and Jessica and Aaron, my two grandchildren, are the loves of my life.

I relish the telling of my story, and I hope you enjoy reading it as much as I've enjoyed sharing it.

Chapter 1
GUMBINNEN: *The Beginning*

In the summer of 1992 I stood with my son Leslie in front of the house in Gumbinnen, in the former East Prussia, Germany, where I was born 87 years ago. Many thoughts went through my mind, especially how my life and that of my family would have turned out had not the seizure of power by the Nazis in 1933, and the ensuing World War II, tragically altered the course of my life as well as that of millions of other people in all of Europe.

Gumbinnen was a small but flourishing administrative center with about 20,000 residents, a large military garrison, and a prosperous middle class. The city was well laid-out. It had direct train connections to the West via Koenigsberg and Berlin and even further to Paris. To the East, the train went via Lithuania (only 20 miles away) to St. Petersburg.

Shortly before the end of the war in 1945, Gumbinnen came under the occupation of Russian troops, which had advanced into East Prussia. Those Germans who had not yet fled were expelled or killed. Today the town is called Gusev and is under Russian administration, but not part of Russia (but *that* is another story!)

Our house was not destroyed during the war, the house in which not only was I born in 1929, but also my father in 1893. Our family lived on the first floor, while my cousin Jochem and his parents lived on the second. The adjacent building (Koenigsstrasse 1, corner Hindenburg-strasse) was our store, founded by my grandfather in 1883. It was a very profitable store. We sold everything from ready-to-wear clothing, high fashion attire, novelties, sports equipment, and toys. The store had about fifty employees.

The two administrators were Freulein Frese and Freulein Horn. My father managed the toy and sports department, and my uncle Heinrich managed all the others. My grandmother sat at the cash register until her death in 1929. I remember going with my cousin Jochem to play at the store after it closed at night. He would chase me around the aisles on his *roller*, a favorite toy. A *roller* is a skate board with a vertical steering column and handle bars. You stand on it with one foot and push off with the other. I would run after him laughing. Jochem was six years older than I and attended the Friedrichs Schule (the public secondary school, called a Gymnasium) which was formerly also attended by Werner von Braun.

As members of a well-to-do German Jewish middle class, we had a very good life in Gumbinnen. Our house was situated in the best neighborhood in town. We regarded ourselves primarily as Germans, although most of our social activities were with other Jewish families. At the time about fifty Jewish families lived in Gumbinnen. The social life of the Jewish community took place at private parties and festivities.

We had a small, rather Orthodox synagogue, in which the women were seated upstairs. Cantor Wasser also acted as our Hebrew teacher and spiritual counselor for the community. We all dutifully attended services on the High Holy Days and celebrated Passover, but that was about the extent of our observance. We considered ourselves good Jews, and I am sure we contributed *tzedaka* to worthy causes.

The only member of our family who was very religious was my paternal grandmother, Cecilia Lindenstraus (nee Friedman), from Berlin, who died the year I was born. Hers must have been an arranged marriage, for how else could a Berliner have met a man from Gumbinnen?

Standing in front of our house in 1992, I said to my son, "I can't help thinking that I would probably still be living here if there had been no Hitler. I might be managing the store. Perhaps by now I would have successfully opened ten stores all over East Prussia and built myself a beautiful new villa." What a different path my life has taken!

Gumbinnen was beautiful. The river Pissa wound its way through our town, and each side of the river was lined with linden trees, which created a canopy over the paths where people often strolled. Everyone was well-dressed. Summers were warm, and we vacationed for many weeks in Kranz on the Baltic Sea near Koenigsberg or in Zoppot, an international resort with elegant hotels and a casino.

My mother, Lille, was born in Danzig, now known as Gdansk and part of Poland. My parents married there on November 4, 1927. My father liked to play tennis in long white pants, as was customary then. I believe he played Jochem's mother, Tante Hansel. He was quite good, I heard.

My mother was a tall, beautiful, and very elegant woman. I suspect she never really felt at home in the provincial Gumbinnen with its lack of social and cultural life. She hardly ever went to the store, but she did not spend her time looking after me, either; that was not customary, anyway. Each child had a governess, and according to my cousin, mine was young and pretty. She dressed me, fed me, played with me, and took me out for walks, and was very important in our lives. It is therefore understandable that children were often closer to their governesses than their own mothers. In retrospect, this was a blessing in disguise, because I did not really miss my mother very much after she was gone.

Once, I was told, my governess and I took a walk along the river and came across an ice cream vendor. I was allowed to buy an ice cream, but only to lick it and spit it out. "You must not swallow, you might get a sore throat," my governess warned me. I was sheltered, cheerful and happy, charming and spoiled, I have heard. I had an incredible amount of toys from our store and a *Kachel Ofen* (a ceramic heater) in my room.

Each family had a live-in maid. Ours was the "thin Berta," to differentiate her from the "fat Berta," my uncle's maid.

My father Louis was very outgoing. He told jokes and performed impromptu skits at dinner parties in Gumbinnen. He was also an excellent whistler. I still remember how he used to whistle marches and operetta tunes to me for hours on end. He also always carried pieces of chocolate in his jacket pocket, and I have adopted this custom. We also share the habit of writing everything down on little slips of paper. And yet I somehow always had the feeling that my father was a humorless man who seldom laughed. I also thought him a bit of a hypochondriac. Jochem assured me, however, that just the opposite was the case.

There was racism and an undercurrent of anti-Semitism even in the 1920s in Gumbinnen. My cousin told me that the store hired a mulatto girl. After she started to work, the fifty employees took a vote and informed my father and uncle that they would all quit if the girl stayed. So my family was forced to let her go.

Our store was the second biggest in Gumbinnen. The largest store, also Jewish-owned, was Dembinsky's. Their general manager was Mr. Sally Kaufmann, and he had an affair with my mother.

The year 1933 was the beginning of the end. In January the Nazis came into power. We were forced to sell our department store and the two buildings (*Zwangsverkauf* means "forced sale") at a fraction of their value, to a Mr. Walter Kraft, later a pilot in the German Air Force. My parents and I moved to Danzig, and my cousin and his parents moved to Konigsberg. My mother started a shirt factory in Danzig. Sally Kaufman naturally moved there, too. I can still remember the shouting matches between my father and mother, which got worse and worse. A year later they separated. My mother moved in with Sally Kaufmann, and she kept the shirt factory.

My parents were divorced in Danzig in August 1936. Looking at the divorce papers, I discovered that under German law, if both parties are found at fault, and both are found guilty in a divorce, a boy stays with the father and a girl with the mother. So that is how I wound up with my father, who lived with me and a housekeeper in a little apartment in Danzig. I went to a Jewish school, and I remember spending my weekends with my mother and Onkel Sally, which is what I called him. I really liked Onkel Sally a lot then, more than my mother, and it is interesting that nearly twenty years later at the airport in Bogotá, Colombia, the only person I recognized was Onkel Sally. Until he died many years later, I continued to call him Onkel Sally. I do not remember exactly when my mother and Sally got married, but it was in Danzig.

In 1938, my mother and Onkel Sally suddenly packed up and left for Colombia, South America to escape the Nazis. I still have an article from the Nazi newspaper called *Danziger Vorposten* dated June 28, 1938 headlined "How the Jews Cheat Their Employees." It alleges that the Jew Kauffmann (my mother), owner of a shirt factory, embezzled money from German citizens, cheating her workers out of their wages and fleeing the country overnight after selling the machines and inventory.

I only remember I hardly had time to say goodbye to her. They chose the Colombian city of Bogotá because my mother's sister, Hertha de Vries, her husband

Hermann, and their daughter Brigitte already lived there, having left Germany eight months earlier. After my mother's departure and the shirt factory's seizure by the state, my father decided to move to Koenigsberg with me to join his brother, Heinrich, and family. Koenigsberg, today called Kaliningrad because it is part of Russia, was the capital of East Prussia.

By then it had become more and more obvious that we would have to leave Germany. In November 1938, we lived through the horror of *Kristallnacht*, the night of broken glass. Thousands of SA and SS men burned 1400 synagogues and Jewish stores throughout Germany, including those in Koenigsberg.

My father spent a lot of time travelling back and forth between Koenigsberg and Danzig, where he kept his savings. He felt they were safer there because Danzig—between the two world wars—had been declared independent and a free city under the Versailles Treaty.

My father decided he had better remarry in order to have someone to take care of me when and if we left Germany. Another Lillie arrived on the horizon. Her last name was Guter, and evidently she already knew my father, having met him some time ago during his business trips from Gumbinnen to Koenigsberg. They met again and married in Koenigsberg in January 1939. I found it amusing that my stepmother's name was the same as my mother's, but that is where the similarity ended. Lillie Guter was short and plump, with a pretty face. She originally came from Zinten, a small village in East Prussia. She was a bookkeeper by profession.

Lillie was very business-oriented. She was also street smart (which later came in very handy), but not educated or sophisticated. Her sister Friedel was married to Isidor Zausmer, a dentist.

For a while I lived with Lillie's parents, David and Ema Guter, in Koenigsberg. I went to a Jewish school in the basement of the big synagogue in Koenigsberg, which was partially burned down on *Kristallnacht*. Once I was beaten up by Nazi kids on the way home. After that, Onkel David, my new step-grandfather, took me to school every morning and picked me up in the afternoon. The beating apparently did not have a great impact on me—I hardly remember it. I do remember sneaking out of the apartment every time I heard the sound of a military band playing march music in the distance, even though my stepmother had forbidden me to leave the apartment by myself.

Once I snuck out when I heard the military bands from my window, and ran two blocks to the main street. The music came closer and closer. Even then, I found march music irresistible. When I got to the main square, the Parade Platz, crowds were already lining both sides of the street. I stood back, waiting for the parade to turn the corner. First came soldiers on horseback, big, black, beautiful East Prussian horses, and then the SA men with their red-and-black swastika armbands. As everybody shouted *"Heil Hitler,"* and *"Sieg Heil,"* and lifted their arms in the Nazi salute, I too had to lift my arm to avoid being conspicuous.

The best part of the parade was the large German Army band. The musicians marched in perfect steps with their trumpets and glockenspiels and many drums of all sizes. Amidst the drums I saw a German shepherd dog pulling a small cart. On the cart was a large Pauke, a big drum that a drummer was beating in good German precision, while the German shepherd dog marched in step with the music and the marchers. What a spectacle! I was absolutely fascinated and in a daze.

To this very day, I get goosebumps when I hear a march, even if it is played by a high school band on New York's Fifth Avenue during the Columbus Day Parade. Whenever I feel sad or feel down, I play my cassettes of German or American marches, and I immediately feel better. How strange, when you consider the Germans were our enemies! After the parade passed, I ran back home, and this time I got caught by Lillie, who had come home early. She severely scolded me, and with good cause. I could very well have been caught watching the parade by the Nazis. Since Jews were not permitted such pastimes anymore, God knows what could have happened to me.

By 1939, almost all of my parents' friends had left Germany. One day, my father and stepmother, as well as my Uncle Heinrich and family, and Lillie's sister and parents, had a long talk about leaving Germany. Few countries still accepted Jewish refugees. There was very little choice. It was impossible to get a visa for the United States. Only two destinations were available to us: Shanghai, which was an open international city for which no visa was required, or the island of Madagascar, off Africa.

I do not know why they chose Shanghai. Probably because we heard that other German Jews had already left for Shanghai. Once the decision was made, preparations began in earnest. They started putting money together, visiting travel agencies, applying for exit permits. Finally, in July of 1939, my father, who was the leader of our little family group, was able to buy ten first class round trip tickets on the SS Scharnhorst, a German luxury liner of the North German Lloyd Steamship Line, which ironically once belonged to a Jew. We were compelled to buy round-trip tickets, even though it was clear we would not return.

Each family was allowed to take a lift (a large 20-foot van or container in which refugees brought out their belongings) filled with furniture, clothes, dishes, crystal, carpets, etc. Later, in Shanghai, the contents of these vans saved many lives because people were able to sell some of their belongings to buy food.

My father managed to send 500 British pounds sterling to a cousin in London, with the agreement that he would send the money to us in Shanghai, since Jews were not allowed to take any money out of Germany. Jews leaving Germany were forced to pay a high "exit tax" and had most of their assets confiscated.

So in July 1939, the ten of us: my father, stepmother, and I; Onkel Heinrich, Tante Hansel and Jochem; Tante Friedel and Onkel Isy; and Lillie's parents, Tante Ema and Onkel David, took a train from Koenigsberg to Bremerhafen via Berlin and set sail for Shanghai. As a ten-year-old, I found the whole thing very exciting. I was still quite a happy child, as far as I can remember, and I really do not recall missing my mother, who was living in Colombia by then. My father and the rest of my family, though, were very nervous when we finally boarded the train. During the trip, SA men constantly boarded the train to examine passports and travel documents. We clutched our first-class round-trip tickets to Shanghai for dear life. In our pockets we also had all the documents needed to travel within Germany, but the Nazis had enough power to arrest anyone, especially Jews, without question.

The train ride seemed endless. My father kept repeating aloud, as if saying it would make it come true, "Once we are on the ship and out of Germany, we will be in excellent shape because I managed to transfer the 500 pounds of the remaining money to my cousin Landsberger in London. So there is no risk of our being caught with money on us. If we had it we would be caught and arrested. Now we will be able to live a good life in Shanghai and, as soon as we can, we will emigrate to a better place." He had given instructions to his cousin Landsberger to transfer the money by wire to Louis Lindenstraus in Shanghai, care of American Express.

After about fifteen hours on the train, miraculously without any encounters with the Nazis, we arrived in Bremerhaufen and boarded the Scharnhorst. The passengers were mostly German Jews, but also other Germans and a few Asians. The ship was beautiful, with luxurious staterooms. There were formal parties nearly every evening. Amazingly, my father and my other relatives managed to pack formal clothes. The food was excellent. We went swimming in the pool, and I really had a ball. As far as I was concerned, it was a fun-filled trip.

In Rotterdam, the first stop, Lillie's cousin, a scientist named Oscar Meirowsky, visited us on the ship to say goodbye and give Lillie a little package containing platinum, which we later sold in Shanghai. This probably got us through a whole year. We then stopped in Genoa, Barcelona, and Port Said, and sailed through the Suez Canal, practically in sight of Palestine. We stopped in India, the Philippines, and Hong Kong, and finally arrived in Shanghai in August 1939, thirty days after leaving Germany.

Not until I was an adult did I realize that my father must have been a genius to get those ten tickets for the Scharnhorst, thereby most certainly saving our ten lives. Once the war broke out in September 1939, the only way to get to Shanghai was first from Italian ports and finally via Russia and Siberia via railroad, and only a trickle of refugees succeeded in making that trip. Ours was the last voyage on the Scharnhorst. Upon her return to Germany, she was converted to a troop ship and was later sunk by the Allies.

I remember standing on deck, seeing the famous Shanghai skyline called "The Bund" as we sailed up the Wang Poo River. The day was brutally hot and humid. We were sweating profusely in our heavy German clothing. We were met by officials of

HIAS (Hebrew International Aid Society), who loaded us onto trucks and took us to an orientation center. My father immediately ran to the American Express office, and indeed found a $100 transfer from his cousin.

He was happy, and we proceeded to rent a small apartment in the French Concession of Shanghai, one of the best neighborhoods in the city. We looked forward to receiving the rest of the money from London and starting a new life in Shanghai.

In spite of my experiences with the Nazis in Koenigsberg, my parents' divorce, and my mother's leaving me, I as a ten-year-old found this whole adventure extremely exciting. Now another major change in my life and that of my family was about to begin.

Chapter 2
A NEW BEGINNING IN SHANGHAI

Our new apartment in Shanghai on the Avenue Joffre in the French Concession was in the neighborhood where the opening scenes of the film *Empire of the Sun* were shot. We did not have to buy any furniture because all we needed was brought over from Germany in our lift. My father and Lillie were enthusiastic about starting a new life in Shanghai. My father now started a correspondence in earnest with his cousin Landsberger in London for the transfer of the rest of the money. He planned to use it to open a business. My father and Lillie actually did open a stand at a market where they sold soaps, perfumes, and other items they had bought from other German refugees. I particularly remember a display of bottles of 4711, a German cologne.

The correspondence between my father and his cousin in England was mainly by telegram because the letters took too long and telegrams could be picked up at the local American Express office. Telegrams kept arriving, but instead of money, they held only excuses and promises. All my father's efforts seemed in vain. By November 1939, it was quite clear that no more money was forthcoming, and the mood in our house was very grim. My stepmother immediately took charge. Strong and down-to-earth, she got us an apartment in Hongkew, a much cheaper Chinese working-class neighborhood in Shanghai.

My father was a broken man. He had worked so hard in Germany and Danzig to put his last savings together and had sent them to England, in spite of the danger of arrest and imprisonment in a concentration camp. That a relative could so betray him was inconceivable to my father. He could not bear it.

With the arrival of winter, the weather in Shanghai became very damp and cold. The wind at the stand in the open market was brutal. My father, who was always extremely health-conscious and always advised me to eat well, take walks, and take deep breaths to get a lot of fresh air, just lost his will to live. He was shattered. In December that year, he developed *Lungenentzuendung* (pneumonia) and was admitted to a hospital. There were no antibiotics in those days, so pneumonia was a serious sickness. He passed away December 21, 1939, four months after we arrived in Shanghai. I was still only ten years old. I said *Kaddish* for him every day for nearly a year, usually after school, at a small Russian synagogue in Hongkew called Congregation Ohel Moishe. We were devastated. I firmly believe that my father could have pulled through, though, had he really wanted to live.

In Hongkew we lived among the 95% of the 18,000 German and Austrian refugees in Shanghai who eventually had to live in Hongkew after 1941 when the Japanese took over the whole city and declared part of Hongkew a ghetto. We were surrounded by other residents: approximately 100,000 Chinese lived with us in Hongkew (or we with them.) Hongkew was an area of approximately forty square blocks. The total population of Shanghai at that time was 5,500,000, or less than half of what it is now. There were about 4,000 Russian Jews in Shanghai who had escaped Russia in 1917 before the revolution, and about 1,000 Sephardic Jews, some of whom had arrived in Shanghai a hundred years ago. They played a large role in our lives.

The Sephardic Jews, originally from Iraq, were very rich. Families like Kadoorie, Sassoon, and Hardoon controlled many of Shanghai's big businesses, such as the electric company, bus company, trading companies, and banks. They were the ones who immediately helped us. One of the tall buildings on Shanghai's waterfront, Sir Victor Sassoon's Embankment Building, was converted into a refugee processing center. Sir Horace Kadoorie, who died in 1995, was the donor of our school, which opened its doors November 1, 1939. Even though the official name of the school was Shanghai Jewish Youth Association School (SJYA), it was lovingly called the Kadoorie School.

The school eventually had 600 students and 17 teachers. It awarded the high school degree, with instruction based on the English school system, and all classes were taught in English. Our headmistress, Mrs. Lucie Hartwich, a German-Jewish educator, made sure all refugee children learned English immediately, which we did— much faster than our parents. We had excellent teachers from all over the world. Even our sports were international—soccer, ping pong (the Chinese national sport), track and field, and boxing.

On Friday nights we conducted our own Shabbat services at school. I was among the students who sang in the choir directed by our Hebrew teacher, Mr. Wesel. To this day, the Friday night service is my favorite. I often attend Friday night services at our synagogue in New York so I can sing *L'cha dodi.*

I was enrolled in the Kadoorie School in November 1939, soon after we moved to Hongkew. Like most of the other kids, I loved the school because it provided us more or less a normal life, which our parents could not give us. My school years were a wonderful experience, except for the last year of high school when my best friend, Gert Kirschner, and I just stopped studying. We had too many outside interests, such as girls, getting jobs, and having a good time. Since we did not do our homework, we knew we would get bad report cards and not be allowed to graduate, so we simply quit school early. To this day I do not have a high school diploma. I did not even keep my report cards because they were so bad. Years later, in New York, when people asked me from which schools I graduated, I always answered with a straight face, "Shanghai High and Shanghai U, of course."

The situation was not all that rosy for our parents. First of all, it was so difficult to get jobs in Hongkew that people had to resort to makeshift jobs to make a living. Those who had saved money opened small stores or restaurants. Lawyers sold newspapers; many people sold their belongings on the street, since most refugees were able to bring lifts with them, loaded with furniture, carpets, crystal, even paintings and household goods. Everything in Shanghai had its price.

Our community offered many social and religious activities. We had High Holy Day services conducted by many rabbis and cantors in rented movie theatres. We had dancing schools, technical schools (to help train people for a new profession), sports clubs, cafes and nightclubs, three daily German newspapers, and even our own German radio station.

Although we lived in a poor section of town and were poor ourselves, and in spite of the unbearable heat, humidity, and dirty conditions in Shanghai, we tried to live as we were accustomed to in Germany. Many refugees never really learned proper English. Hardly anyone spoke Chinese. We spoke German at home, and we communicated with the Chinese in Pidgin English, a slang, adequate for trading, or rather, bargaining. Nothing was ever bought or sold without bargaining.

When you entered a small refugee apartment, it looked just like it did in Germany: bulky furniture and Meissner porcelain and silver cutlery. The food, even though cooked on a small Chinese charcoal stove on the roof, was German-style. The stove had only one burner and had to be continually fanned. The outhouse was also on the roof garden. There was no kitchen or running water in most of the dwellings in Hongkew. I don't think I had one single Chinese meal in Shanghai during the war. We did not have money for restaurants, and even if we had been able to go out, I am sure we would have gone to a German restaurant. I always bought boiled hot sweet potatoes on the street, a very tasty, nutritious, and cheap staple. They were especially good in the winter because you could roll the hot potatoes in your hands to keep them warm. I ate so many sweet potatoes that it was fifty years before I could eat sweet potatoes again at Thanksgiving in New York.

My uncle Isy and his wife Friedl (sister of my stepmother), had a better life than most refugees in Shanghai. Isy was a dentist with a practice in the Japanese section of town. I visited them often, particularly because, having no children of their own, they loved to spoil me. They were also better off financially than any of us. In addition to a lot of jewelry, which he made himself, Onkel Isy was able to take with him his complete dental practice, all of his equipment, even the dental chair. I do not remember if he purposely set up his practice in the Japanese section of Shanghai or if it was a coincidence. There, he was able to attract many Japanese patients who could afford to pay him. The Japanese loved him, but I do not know if they loved him because he was a good dentist or because he was German.

Onkel Isy lived in an apartment on the second floor of a four-story walk-up. It was well-kept and clean. All the other tenants were Japanese, and I used to play with the Japanese children in the hall and outside the house. I was able to speak a few words of Japanese that we learned in school. Every school in Shanghai was obligated to teach Japanese, including ours. We learned the basics as well as the modern Japanese alphabet, called *hiragana* (a, e, i, o, u, etc.)

I often stayed overnight with Onkel Isy, Tante Friedl, and Tante Emma, her mother, who also lived with them. The apartment was quite large. When you entered you were in a small waiting room for patients that led into the treatment room where Onkel Isy saw patients. There was another small adjoining room where he did his lab work. I remember helping him work with the cement he used to make impressions of teeth. He used my mouth as a model for making these impressions. When the cement got hard, he and I worked on it with a knife, carving out the teeth. I loved it. On the other side of the apartment, in another large room at the back, all three family members slept and lived. It was divided by a large hanging carpet for privacy. They also had a bathroom and a kitchen with running water, which was a luxury.

Onkel Isy got special permission to stay out of our ghetto, even after 1943 when all refugees had to move to Hongkew by order of the Japanese army, simply because he had Japanese patients and connections. But in 1944 even they had to move to the ghetto. They bought a small house on Wayside Road, where he continued his practice. The office was downstairs, and he lived upstairs. I visited there often, too, but by then Onkel Isy had become very stingy. My cousin Jochem told me that Onkel Isy employed him in his lab to teach him to become a dental technician, but never paid him one penny, not even for bus fare. Finally, Jochem's mother told him he could not work there any more. Thus ended Jochem's career as a dental technician. To me, however, Onkel Isy and the rest of his family were generous and welcoming. The whole family always treated me like their own and loved me. I felt very lucky in that respect.

My stepmother slowly adjusted to losing my father. In spite of the lack of money, she did an excellent job coping. Down-to-earth, organized, and a hard worker, she even managed to save some money. She got a job in a deli, which not only helped our expenses, but also allowed her to bring home some food. Even in Shanghai it was possible to buy German cold cuts such as salami, head cheese (*suelze*), sausages, cheese, and good bread. Butter was not available, but we had margarine and pork fat. I remember enjoying everything sweet, which is true to this day. I always put sugar on my spinach and carrots, and I spread margarine and sugar or chocolate on my bread. Recently an East Prussian friend told me it was customary there to eat sweet dishes, which is probably the source of my cravings for sweets.

Our first home in Hongkew was a nice, single room, which Lillie and I shared. She took excellent care of me, although she could be quite strict and tough with me. Only now can I fully appreciate that. She had a few boyfriends, and their company helped me too.

As the years passed, times got tougher for us in Hongkew. First of all, in 1943 the Japanese army officially declared that all 18,000 of the German and Austrian refugees (they referred to us as "stateless") had to move into the ghetto. Jobs and living conditions got worse and worse. People had little left to sell, and a few thousand of those who could no longer support themselves had to move into the *Heime* (camps.) These *Heime* were run by the refugee organizations with help from HIAS. Since there was no rent to pay, single people lived in large barracks, and families, like my friend Gert and his parents, in rooms as small as closets, with bunk beds in which you could barely turn around. Cooking was done outdoors, in front of each room. Bathrooms were communal; there was no running water. The HIAS camps had soup kitchens and mess halls where meals were cooked and served. On the other hand, the camps also had concerts, operettas, comedians, and theatre. Lillie and I were fortunate in never having to move into a camp because she somehow always provided for us, even during the worst of years.

My friend Gert was in my class, and we did everything together: after school sports, chasing girls, playing games. Once we even had a real fistfight in the schoolyard. Lillie's mother, who I called Tante Ema, once gave me a book called *Die Deutschen Helden* (Tales of German Heros) that contained stories about Siegfried and the dragon, Brunhilde, and Dietrich and his apprentices. I loved that book and read it many times. Gert and I acted out many of the scenes. Once, in our little room, we grabbed brooms for spears, masked our heads with sieves, and covered ourselves with old skirts. We put stools on the bed, then perched on them, and using the dialogue from the book, tried to push each other off the bed with the brooms. This led to mass destruction and crashes. One day Lillie came home from work early, and seeing the mess, gave us hell, screaming like a madwoman.

Another time we had a school outing to a public swimming pool in Jessfeld Park outside our district. Some teachers drove us in a truck. It was very hot and muggy, so we spent the whole day in the pool. When it was time to assemble for the return trip, Gert and I stayed behind. We did not hear the signal that it was time to go (or we did not want to hear it), so we stayed for a few more hours, and I got the worst sunburn of my life. It hurt so much that I could not put on my shirt. We had no way of getting home. There were no telephones, so we had no choice but to start walking, and eventually we were picked up by a Japanese army truck. The Japanese soldiers had a reputation of being cruel, but on the other hand, they were usually very nice to children. We were very scared. They asked us where we lived and delivered each of us to our respective homes. In the meantime, my stepmother, worried stiff by our lateness, ran over to Gert's house to see if he was home or if his mother had heard anything. When his mother said no, Lillie had a tremendous outburst and blamed all my wrongdoings on Gert and his mother. They had a big fight in German of course, and Lillie and Gert's mother did not talk to each other for a long time. As my sunburn got worse and worse, the skin on my back came off in strips, and I had to sleep on my stomach for a whole week. Lillie never really punished me for being late—I guess she figured the pain was enough punishment.

Tropical diseases were rampant. After 1943 it was difficult to obtain medicines because the Japanese barred passage of shipments sent by American relief organizations. All forms of diarrhea, stomach ailments, typhoid, cholera, and malaria and jaundice were common among us.

The sanitary conditions were terrible. Altogether, 1,581 of our people died in Shanghai between 1939 and 1945, many from tropical diseases. Since people had no running water, it had to be bought from street vendors: hot water was for washing and cold water for cooling, and, supposedly, clean water for drinking. The water had to be boiled. Even then, we were never sure that we would not get sick. Water was sold by coolies who walked from lane to lane and house to house, with two large bamboo containers secured by ropes and connected to a bamboo stick, which they carried on their shoulders, a bucket on each side. The Chinese were masters of carrying large and heavy loads on their shoulders, always on a bamboo stick with the load balanced on the side of the shoulder. Vendors came through the lanes yelling, "wasser, wasser!" They learned more German words than we did Chinese. When we heard them yelling, we ran out with our own bucket to buy our water. After much bargaining, the man would fill our bucket.

I became a bar mitzvah in Shanghai in June 1942, in the same Russian synagogue in Hongkew, Congregation Ohel Moishe on Ward Road, where I said *kaddish* for my father three years earlier. I remember very little about my bar mitzvah except that women sat upstairs and the officiating rabbi was *Prediger* Kohn from Germany. I read my speech in German. Lillie gave me my father's *tallis* (prayer shawl) as a present. She embroidered my initials on a piece of silk and sewed it over my father's initials on the *tallis* bag. I still have the *tallis* and wear it every year at the High Holy Days services.

Lillie met a man called Henry (Heinz) Gerson from Berlin, and they got married in Shanghai in 1944, by which time the situation in Hongkew had become pretty desperate. Heinz was a good husband to Lillie and a companion to me. He was a kind person, always gentle with Lillie, who was not the easiest person to get along with. The three of us lived together in half a room, separated by hanging Persian carpet, which we brought from Germany. I must have been about fifteen years old then, and, of course, already horny. (We boys used to get together to read dirty books, including

The Autobiography of a Flea.) Sometimes I woke up in the middle of the night and heard Lillie and her husband making love.

Sometime during that period I got malaria and jaundice. We had no antibiotics. I had an attack every six hours with such regularity that I could set my watch by it. Walking on the street, I would look at my watch and think, I'd better go home now—its only half an hour to my next attack. These attacks were either a severe form of hot flashes with fever during which Lillie had to wrap me in cold towels, or shivering cold attacks in which several down comforters and wool blankets did not keep me from shaking all over. Only Lillie's two hot water bottles against my skin helped a little. These attacks lasted at least a year. Finally, the refugee doctors received a drug called Atabrine, which cured me. Many years later, shortly after my arrival in New York in 1953, my history of malaria kept me out of the army during the Korean War.

We moved several times in Hongkew. One of the last places we lived was a house whose second floor consisted of one room, again divided by that Persian rug. The three of us lived in one half and a Viennese couple in the other half. Downstairs, a large Chinese family lived with their children, grandchildren, cats, dogs, and chickens. We had no real contact with them. We said hello and so did they, and that was it. Upstairs, one floor above ours, was a small roof garden where we hung the laundry to dry and where we cooked our meals on a little charcoal stove which we constantly had to fan to keep hot. On the roof was also a tiny cubicle containing a bucket in which we all (the two European families) had to relieve ourselves. Once a day, a Chinese coolie came through our room to the roof to pick up the full bucket and replace it with an empty one.

Many years later, my stepmother, who then lived in Monroe, Louisiana, never tired of telling the story of how the coolie invariably timed his visit just as we were eating and how he sometimes hit the stairs with the bucket, spilling some of the contents. You can imagine the unbelievable smell (stink is a better word!) After that, we could never finish our meal. Coolies wore large straw hats and wide straw skirts to protect themselves against the torrential rains. With these clumsy outfits, no wonder they used to bump against the stairs, which went right through our room. But we took everything in stride, never losing an opportunity for a laugh. What else could we do?

When she told the story, Lillie laughed so hard that she could never finish it, but it did not matter because her friends in Monroe had heard that story many, many times before.

Gert and I joined a British Boy Scout troop that was originally exclusively for English boys, but later expanded to include refugee boys. The Thirteenth Troupe in Hongkow was only for us, and although well-organized, it functioned underground because no British organization was allowed to exist during the Japanese occupation. We had weekly meetings, parties, and even uniforms. We studied and were awarded badges for special skills. I became Assistant Patrol Leader. We went on hikes and camped overnight during summer. It was another great way to keep us busy and to teach us something. After the war, we each received a medal stating that we served in the Boy Scouts under Japanese occupation. I still have my medal. We kids were always in high spirits and busy, even during the toughest years, 1944 and 1945.

Then in 1945, the American Air Force began bombing Shanghai and neighboring cities. Many a day, we saw the B-29s flying overhead on their bombing missions to other locations. Air raid sirens usually sounded after the planes had already gone by—that is how poorly the system worked. We were never too concerned because we believed that the Americans knew we were in Hongkew and would therefore not bomb our district. The Japanese knew it too and built radio stations and other sophisticated installations right in our district. So on July 17, 1945, the Americans actually did bomb Hongkew. Forty-five refugees and many hundreds of Chinese people were killed. I was already working at my first job in a weaving factory when I heard the bombs and sirens. I ran home, only to find Lillie on the roof, hanging up the wash. I yelled for her to get down, but she stayed up there until every piece of laundry was hung. That attack gave us a real jolt; now we were all very scared. After the war, we learned from American pilots that they knew exactly where we were, but had orders to bomb our ghetto anyway. They had delayed the bombing as long as they could. During one of the air raids they dropped a leaflet geared to the allied prisoners of war, saying, "Attention Allied Prisoners," indicating the end was near, and signed by General Wedemeyer. I picked up that leaflet and saved it.

ATTENTION
ALLIED PRISONERS

Allied Prisoners of War and Civilian Internees, these are your orders and/or instructions in case there is a capitulation of the Japanese forces:

1. You are to remain in your camp area until you receive further instructions from this headquarters.

2. Law and order will be maintained in the camp area.

3. In case of a Japanese surrender there will be allied occupational forces sent into your camp to care for your needs and eventual evacuation to your homes. You must help by remaining in the area in which we now know you are located.

4. Camp leaders are charged with these responsibilities.

5. The end is near. Do not be disheartened. We are thinking of you. Plans are under way to assist you at the earliest possible moment.

(Signed) A. C. WEDEMEYER
Lieutenant General, U. S. A.
Commanding

Chapter 3

LIFE IN HONGKEW

The Garden Bridge divided Hongkew and the International Settlement Section where all commerce and business took place and important stores such as Wing On were located. Today, the store is called "Number One Department Store," and Nanking Road, where the store is located, is called Nanjing Road. The famous race course with the infamous sign "No Chinese and no dogs" was on the continuation of Nanking Road, known as Bubbling Well Road. Today a large housing complex stands in its place.

During the Japanese occupation, starting in 1938, Japanese soldiers stood guard on the Garden Bridge. Chinese people who crossed the bridge had to bow in front of these guards. If they did not bow deep enough, they were hit with a rifle; more than once someone was stabbed with a bayonet and tossed in the river below.

American, British, and other Allied citizens were interned in regular civilian prisoner-of-war camps on the outskirts of Shanghai. We heard that they were treated badly. It is unclear to me why we Jewish refugees were treated relatively well by our Japanese captors, especially since the Nazis, through their German embassy, pressured the Japanese to harm us. I recently read that the Nazis had a plan they were trying to sell to the Japanese: take all the refugees, load them onto ships, sail out to the ocean, and sink the ships. There were also rumors that the Japanese were building gas ovens to kill us and that mass graves were being dug to bury us. Fortunately, that didn't happen.

But the grownups became sicker and weaker from malnutrition and the famous *Sprue*, a chronic intestinal disease. Times were bad. B-29 bombers flew over Shanghai every day, although there were no more bombing attacks. Just hearing the planes rattled our nerves.

Our ghetto in Hongkew did not have distinct boundaries or walls, just a designated area with signs on certain corners. There were no Japanese guards or soldiers, but if one of us was caught outside our district without the proper pass, swift punishment followed, often beatings or even a jail sentence. A number of refugees died while imprisoned at Garden Bridge Tower jail.

Ironically, our community was forced to organize its own police force, patrol the streets leading out of our district, and check the refugees who crossed the unmarked so-called border. This led to many problems among refugees, even fistfights, because sometimes if papers were not in order, one refugee had to turn in another. Many refugees stood in line from five in the morning at the offices of our famous or infamous Major Goya to try to obtain this valuable pass to leave the district. You could see proud German Jews standing in orderly lines in their heavy German clothes, sweating in the sun. Sometimes people fainted from the heat. When their turn finally came, Major Goya lectured and humiliated them and very often withheld their passes. All children who attended the Kadoorie School also needed passes to go to school, since it was located outside the district. We were given permanent passes, which we wore around our necks in little pouches. Lillie had given me an American $20 bill, which she put into that pouch and which I was supposed to use in the utmost emergency. I never had to use it.

When my best friend, Gert Kirschner, and I dropped out of high school, half a year before graduation, Gert got a job as an apprentice tanner, and I got a job with a large silk weaving and dyeing factory. It was called Dandy and was owened by Russian Jews. Stands of raw silk were washed in a hot liquid to soften them, and then dyed in many different colors. We dyed silk by holding the strands of silk in our hands and submerging them in the dye for quite a long time. These strands were very heavy when wet, and the smell and vapors were unhealthy for our lungs. When we dyed silk blue, my hands turned blue. When I first came home with blue hands, Lillie thought they were frozen. She got very upset. Even though the work was physically exhausting, I enjoyed it. Once the strands were softened and dyed, we put them on weaving stools and Chinese workers wove them by hand. They used the jacquard system in which patterns are on cards with holes, which the weaver must change continuously. The machines made a racket, since for every row the weaver had to push a little boat with the thread through the machine and then slam the cam down to solidify the silk cloth. I never got a chance to actually weave.

I knew the war was nearing an end because of the leaflet I had found. September 3, 1945 marked the end of our ghetto. We knew that the Japanese had lost the war because we were always listening to short wave radios, even though the Japanese had strictly forbidden it. That day, the Japanese soldiers simply vanished during the night, but not before Major Goya was thoroughly beaten up by some refugees. We were deathly afraid that the vacuum created by the Japanese departure would bring about complete chaos. We feared plundering and killing by the Chinese because there was no real Chinese police force. The Americans had not yet arrived.

In spite of this dangerous situation, my friend Gert and I ventured out of the district on foot into the center of the city, which we had not seen for years. It was a little crazy, but we were adventurous and young. We saw plenty. The Chinese, who had suffered the most from the Japanese, were celebrating. Firecrackers went off, we saw opium dens with Chinese men lying in bunks puffing away. Brothels had recently opened everywhere, eagerly awaiting American servicemen.

We waited anxiously for the Americans to arrive. Finally, after a few days in September, the first Navy ships sailed up the Wang Poo River and thousands of sailors came ashore, turning the city upside down. These guys had two years' pay in their pockets, and Shanghai was an open city. Shanghai immediately adapted and offered sailors anything they were looking for.

Then the Army and Air Force arrived, and with that, help for the refugees. We received all kinds of medicines and food from the Americans. During Chanukah, children received Chanukah *gelt*, which consisted of an envelope with an American dollar inside and the inscription, "An American dollar from An American Jewish soldier." (These were presents from the Jewish Welfare Board.) Many refugees were able to get jobs as civilian employees with the Armed Forces. Although these jobs did not pay well, they gave us access to the Army PX's where we were able to buy everything we had not had for years, such as butter, chocolate, peanut butter, etc.

I immediately quit my job at the weaving factory and started to work for the Army as a messenger boy. The best part for me was that I got an Army bike, of which I was very proud. It was also useful. After a few months, I was promoted to clerk and got a desk job.

We had good times then, and we made lots of friends among the American servicemen. My stepmother and her husband befriended a Jewish sailor from Baltimore. We kept in touch with him and his wife until he died a few years ago. To this day, we get Jewish New Year cards from his widow. Quite a few refugees benefited tremendously from the Army. Many started businesses such as carting away garbage, a popular business because it was well-known that Americans threw out useful things. In Shanghai, everything had a value.

As soon as the war ended, I heard from my mother in Bogotá, and we started corresponding. It became clear she wanted me to go to Colombia, but I had no desire to go there. Of course, my stepmother and her husband tried to convince me in any way they could that it was not necessary for me to leave them to rejoin my natural mother. On the other hand, I had some relatives in Shanghai on my mother's side whom my mother contacted. These people, with whom I was friendly, also started to work on me, pushing me and admonishing me that "blood is thicker than water." "You only have one mother," they said, "and she is sick for you. You have an obligation to go to Bogotá to be with your mother." It was a tug-of-war between those relatives and Lillie, who wanted me to stay with her. I really don't remember where my feelings stood in the conflict, but apparently something told me I had to go to my mother.

Finally, at the beginning of 1947, my mother sent me a ticket for passage to Colombia, and I went, leaving my stepmother broken-hearted. She loved me and treated me like her own son and did not want to lose me, but in the end, she did give in. I had to promise her that if she and Henry emigrated to the United States, I would come and visit them. So on March 2, 1947, at the age of 17, I sailed on the SS General Gordon, a converted American troop ship, to San Francisco. I believe I was among the first refugees to leave Shanghai after the war.

I was very excited standing at the railing of the ship, waving goodbye to my stepmother and her husband, sailing alone into the new world and starting a new life. I was not nervous or apprehensive, apparently ready for whatever the world had to offer me. Hours after we left, we sailed into the Yellow Sea, and most passengers became seasick. But I did not. On the contrary, in my first letter to Lillie from the ship, I described the meals in detail and how much I ate. For breakfast for instance, we got two eggs, porridge, cake and coffee. We stood in line with our trays and were served, then sat down at long tables in the dining hall. We all travelled tourist class, sleeping in bunk beds. My friend Alex was my neighbor. We had people of many nationalities on board, including Chinese, Canadians, English, and Russians. The Chinese slept in their own hall. There were, of course, many refugees, families with kids my own age, and we spent most of our time together in the stern of the ship.

We stopped in Kobe and Yokohama, Japan to take on more passengers, including American servicemen and their families. We were not allowed to disembark in Japan, but we saw the tremendous destruction in both cities, as well as sunken ships in the harbors with only their masts sticking out of the water.

Everything American attracted me, and I became friendly with an American couple. I was fascinated with American jazz. Almost every night an American soldier played jazz on a piano. On the ship I had a wonderful time. I had no one to tell me what to do and when to do it. I was free as a bird. All the single guys were in a big bunk, and we had fun from morning to night.

One night in the middle of the Pacific Ocean on the way to San Francisco, we were awakened by the wailing of sirens. When I got up on deck, our ship was in the middle of a spectacular rescue operation. Another ship had broken in two, and several men were desperately clinging to one of the broken sections. Nothing much could be done at night, the sea was very rough and visibility was poor. Searchlights were trained on the shipwreck, and another ship approached. We heard that we were going to try to rescue the stranded men in the morning. We were so excited that we could hardly sleep that night. We all got up as soon as it was light and saw ten men still clinging to half the ship. A lifeboat was lowered, but the sea was too rough for it to make any headway. Then the ship that had appeared in the night, which was smaller than ours, lowered a lifeboat and actually picked up sailors and brought them over to our ship.

It took some time and effort to hoist them up by ropes, and several men fell back into the water. Eventually, they were all brought on board with only minor injuries. We had a doctor on board and a small hospital. Because of the delay, we did not stop in Honolulu, a city I had hoped to see. As soon as we arrived in San Francisco, reporters boarded the ship and asked if anyone had taken photographs of the rescue operation, offering large amounts of money. Like everybody else, I had taken a lot of rescue photographs, but I did not think my pictures would come out, so I did not offer my roll of film. Later, when my film was developed in San Francisco, I was surprised and angry at myself because my pictures were as good as the best that I had seen in the newspaper. As a matter of fact, a picture that appeared on the front page of a San Francisco newspaper was identical to one I took.

I was extremely excited and impressed as we sailed under the Golden Gate Bridge on our arrival to San Francisco. I went through customs without any trouble. HIAS had people at the dock to help us, and I was put up at the Statler Hilton Hotel on Ellis Street. In my letter home to Lillie, I said, "The hotel was not the best!" It is hard to believe that from my limited experience I knew the difference between a so-so hotel and a luxurious one. I described San Francisco in glowing terms, "The city is all lit up at night—skyscrapers, restaurants, food stores, etc. etc."

I met my second best friend from Shanghai, Hans Freddy, in my hotel lobby. We spent a lot of time together, sightseeing, going to the zoo, visiting Golden Gate Park, and just enjoying the most beautiful city in the world. I also met distant relatives. My transit visa allowed me to stay in the United States for 30 days, until April 20, 1947. HIAS helped me get my visa for Colombia, which took ages. Just four days before the transit visa was due to expire, we asked for an extension and were told that it was not possible. I was supposed to take a train from San Francisco to Miami and then a plane to Colombia. Suddenly, everything was rushed, and on the 16th of April, I got a call at my hotel that my papers were ready and that I would depart by plane the next morning. The time in San Francisco passed too fast. I quickly packed and got ready. At 7:50 AM on April 17th, I left on a United Airlines flight. It was my first time in the air.

Here is a translation of part of a letter I wrote in German on April 17, 1947, on a DC-3 on my way from San Francisco to Miami:

Dear Lillie and Henry,

I left San Francisco this morning at 7:50 AM. We just left Salt Lake City. Salt Lake City is in Utah, and this is the third stop. The first stop was Sacramento, and then Reno, Nevada, and I will arrive in Chicago at 10:30 AM. I will have four hours in Chicago, and then I will fly to Miami for six hours. On the 19th of April, I will leave for Barranquilla, Colombia, and will stay overnight, then fly to Bogotá on the 20th, arriving at 12:35 PM. I think this is quite a trip. I was only allowed to take 55 pounds of luggage. Everything else went by ship. I took Heinz's suitcase and my briefcase, which together weighed 55 lbs. In the suitcase I packed my good suit and all other necessary things. I will send you this letter from Chicago. Nothing else important happened in San Francisco. I went to Golden Gate Park with Goldsteins. I also forgot to tell you that I could have had a job in Frisco through Mr. Greenebaum in his office for $200.00 a month, which would have been nice. In the meantime I like all the flying. You don't feel the takeoff at all, and the landings very little. We just made another stop in Cheyenne, Wyoming. I will not be able to write more to Shanghai if you leave there on May 23. Write me in Colombia, so that I know.

I will write you another letter from Miami. Best regards to the Zaumers. In the meantime I just had a sandwich and some milk. Many regards and kisses, your FLIGHT CAPTAIN GERD VON LINDENSTRAUS. PS. Excuse me for writing with a pencil, but the ink in my pen just ran out. It is now 8 AM, and we are stopping in Des Moines, and will arrive in Chicago at 10:35 AM. I slept well and had an excellent breakfast on board.

My next letter to Lillie and Henry is written from Bogotá on May 14th, about three weeks after I arrived. Here is a translation of some interesting excerpts:

We had four hours in Chicago. I took a bus into the city for $1.00 each way to take a look at the city. You know how I am. Why should I sit at the airport for four hours? I had plenty of addresses in my little book and found that Captain Badesch, one of the officers I worked for as a civilian employee, lived there. I called and spoke to his sister, but he, unfortunately, was out. So I took the Eastern Airlines bus to the *center of town where I spent three hours. First I walked around, and then, to my own amazement, I took the SUBWAY for a short distance. After all, I had not seen a subway in a long time.* [Note: I had never seen a subway.] *I did not dare go too far, in case I got lost. Chicago is a tremendously large city with many tall buildings, much bigger than San Francisco. After all, it is the second-largest city in the U.S. I still like San Francisco better. Then I ate something and wanted to go to a movie, but there was not enough time. I went to a few department stores but did not buy anything, except for three records. You remember, Mammie* [as I called my mother in German], *told me that she has an electric record player, so I bought three records, jazz music, hot stuff. With all that I still got to the bus stop 20 minutes early for the trip back to the airport. I met a family traveling to Venezuela. They had been on the ship with me from Shanghai, so we flew together, and I had someone to talk to. But I also talked to many Americans. We flew five and one half hours nonstop to Miami. I got myself a window seat with a great view. The weather was perfect. I was sitting with a man who, although not Jewish himself, worked with many Jews in the real estate business and is one of the richest men in Chicago. He has a summer house and a boat in Miami and goes there three times a week to see his family. He gave me his card and asked me to write him if I needed anything. You never know.*

The food on the plane was excellent. They even had magazines. A lady from the Jewish Women's League met us in Miami and took us right to the Pan American ticket office. I tried to change my ticket so I would not have to stay overnight in Barranquilla, but the man said that has to be confirmed in Barranquilla. So we stayed in a hotel in Miami and left the next morning at 7 AM for Barranquilla. The heat in Miami was quite different from Shanghai, but I did not get to see anything of the city. Now we flew the biggest plane yet, it had 65 passengers and stopped twice. First in Cuba, where I heard Spanish for the first time, and then in Jamaica. We had a good flight and arrived well in Barranquilla, thank God. I immediately checked to see if I could fly to Bogotá the same day, and they said that they would have to let me know if there is a plane. There was no plane, so I left the next morning. I stayed in a fairly good hotel. The food was miserable. The town was dirty, Just like Shanghai, and very hot. There was even a man from HIAS at the airport who helped me.

So after leaving Shanghai and getting a small but very strong taste of the United States, which was to become my future home, I left for Bogotá and a reunion with my mother. Another very important phase in my young life was about to begin.

Chapter 4

BOGOTÁ, THE FIRST YEARS

I was 17 years old, traveling by myself to a new country, encountering Spanish, a language I did not understand, and about to meet my mother, whom I barely remembered after ten years of separation.

Here I quote from a letter to Lillie:

I arrived in Bogotá April 20th, 1947, at 11:00 AM. Everybody was at the airport. Mammie, Onkel Sally, Tante Herta, Onkel Herman and Brigitte, and many friends of Mammie's. I recognized only Onkel Sally. Mammie looks very different from the picture I had. Brigitte has red hair and not blonde as we thought. She is a very nice girl.

I then describe Bogotá and the apartment, but give no indication of any feeling or emotion upon seeing my mother again. Nor do I do so in another letter. I describe Bogotá:

Some areas are very nice and clean with beautiful streets, also the one where Mammie lives, but there are also neighborhoods as dirty as in Shanghai. Mammie has a flat with four rooms, very modern, as in San Francisco, and they have a delicatessen, where they also sell wines liquor. The store is right next to the building, small, but nice. The city has 350,000 inhabitants and streetcars and buses, which are crowded as in Shanghai. We have a beautiful view of the mountains surrounding Bogotá. So far I have not felt the altitude. The weather is nice, not too hot or cold.

Upon my arrival at the Bogotá airport, everybody hugged and cried, and, of course, we spoke in German. Of the little I remember about that dramatic and emotional reunion, I do recall that I addressed my mother as *Sie*, which is the formal form of address in German. I should have said *du* to her, which is the informal way of saying "you," and which is the way children address their parents. Although in her early forties, my mother already had light gray and white hair, supposedly from worrying about me during the war years. According to my cousin Brigitte, my mother worried herself sick over me for years and talked about me incessantly. She was a tall and beautiful woman. Her gray hair made her look even more elegant. She wore fashionable clothes, made for her by a dressmaker, and she was the belle of every party.

My mother was not well. She suffered from all kinds of pains and attacks, which were well publicized in the family. Everybody had to cater to her. She always got her every wish. Not only was she the head of the whole family and the dominant one, she was also the most social, by far the strongest, and the most spoiled. I did not think she was a very caring person. If things did not go her way, she got an "attack," went to bed, took some pills, and was given an injection by her husband. She was then angry at whomever had dared to disagree with her, and sometimes she did not speak to a family member or friend for weeks or months. I wonder sometimes if these injections were some kind of addictive painkiller. With all that, my mother was very popular in our family and large circle of friends.

And so my new life in Bogotá began. Because we were so high in the mountains (about 8,500 feet above sea level), the mornings and evenings were quite cold, about 30 to 40 degrees Fahrenheit, but during the day, especially when the sun shone, the temperature climbed to about 70 degrees. The air was thin, and walking fast or going up stairs was a little cumbersome; you felt your heart pounding. As a matter of fact, when people arrived in Bogotá from the "hot country" (*tierra caliente*, as it was called in Spanish), or from another city, they were told to lie in bed for a day to take it easy and get accustomed to the high altitude.

People in Bogotá, even the poorest, were rather conservative and well-dressed. Middle and upper-class Colombians dressed very formally, the men mostly in a black hat and umbrella, just in case of rain, and black suits just in case they had to go to a funeral. At night, everybody wore overcoats. The middle class was well-educated, and the Spanish spoken in Bogotá was considered the best and purest in all of South America. The dominant religion was Catholicism. The church was very powerful and influential. Most people had no idea what a Jew was. If you told anyone that Jesus was born Jewish, they would refuse to believe you.

We lived in a comfortable three-bedroom apartment of a four-story walk-up building in an upper-middle-class neighborhood called *Teusaquillo*, a ten-minute walk from the center of the city. Most German Jews lived in that neighborhood or the next one, *Chapinero*. My mother and Onkel Sally had only German-Jewish friends, and all their socializing was with other German and Austrian Jews. There were three quite separate Jewish communities in Bogotá. Ours, the German-Jewish community, was the smallest, comprised of about 500 people, mostly well-off owners of medium-sized stores and other businesses. We had our own congregation, which met in a small house. During the High Holy Days we rented a movie theatre in our neighborhood. There was no rabbi, but we had a permanent cantor named Kamm. The larger, wealthier Polish and Russian community had at least 1,000 members. The Sephardic community, which also had about 1,000 members, kept mostly to itself. The Sephardic Jews were by far the wealthiest, owning factories, department stores, and large wholesale businesses. The three groups hardly ever socialized or intermingled. Each community had its own synagogue, activities, and cemetery.

Intermarriage with Colombian Catholic women was most frequent among men of the German-Jewish community. German Jews spoke only German to each other, and many of them spoke only enough Spanish to get by in business or as necessary. Our lives were completely German-oriented. We ate German food, we had German-Hebrew prayer books, gave German-style parties, and played German card games like *Gottes Segen* by *Kohn*, and *Skat*. The former is a game in which one person is the dealer and one buys cards from one deck. Then the dealer deals from the other deck, and if the cards that he dealt match the cards you bought, you get a pay-out of up to nine times the amount you bet. Bridge was also popular. My mother and Onkel Sally were very good bridge players and had games at least three times a week.

Although my mother was aloof, formal, and self-centered, I got along with her very well. While I was by far her favorite person, I do not think we had a mother-and-son relationship. My family was not at all intellectual or religious. Most of their social life consisted of parties and reunions, many vacations within the country and abroad, but very little culture. I do not remember my relatives going to concerts or operas. They did read novels, but only in German.

I began to fit in very well, and without any problems, to my recollection. About six months after I arrived, we moved to a nice European-style brick house about half a block away. My Onkel Georg (Sally's brother, who was a bachelor), and I both had our own rooms upstairs. My mother and Sally had the master bedroom, also on the second floor. We had two live-in maids, Carmen and Concha, a cook, and a housekeeper. I became very friendly with both of them. I began to learn Spanish through my first circle of friends who, although all German and Austrian, spoke to each other in perfect Spanish.

My mother and Onkel Sally owned a store called *Almacen Kaufmann* (the Kaufmann Store.) It was a glorified and elegant delicatessen, very small, but fully stocked with delicacies from Russian caviar to Hellman's mayonnaise and Scotch whisky. Six girls worked at the counter, joined by Sally and Georg in the peak hours from 5 PM to 7 PM. The store was located at Carrera 17 between Calle 33 and 34, one block from our house. They imported a lot of the delicacies themselves from the United States, Germany, and France and stored them in a small warehouse, which was a big garage around the corner from the store. We sold German-style cold cuts made by German and Swiss-owned sausage factories in Bogotá, and fresh German rolls and rye breads. There was also quite a large German non-Jewish community who were also our customers, as were the Colombians. Most of our customers, however, were German and Austrian Jews. People ordered by telephone, and we delivered. Many good customers had charge accounts, which were paid once a month. Each customer had a little notebook with his name on it, and each purchase was recorded. Onkel Sally and Onkel George personally made all the entries and added them up without adding machines. Eventually I did it too, and thus learned how to add fast and accurately without the aid of any machines. I am still good at it.

It was a prosperous business, and for all I could gather, they made a very good living. My mother did not work at the store, but definitely was the boss and usually graced the store with her presence during peak hours, mainly to say hello and socialize with the customers, most of whom she knew personally.

At 7 AM every day of the week, Sally opened the store with two employees. My Onkel Georg came to relieve Sally, who went home and took a nap every day after lunch and then came back to the store for the peak hours until closing at 8 PM. It was not easy. We were open every day except Sunday afternoon. I started working usually from 9 AM until 6 PM, but my hours were rather flexible and accommodated my rather extensive social life. I worked behind the counter and learned how to slice salami, corned beef, and cheese. I remember a woman came to the store and ordered a half a pound of assorted cold cuts, "*duen geschnitten, es ist fuer den Besuch*," which means, "sliced thin, it is for our guests."

I did not particularly like the work, but I always had time to be with my new friends. My first group of friends in Bogotá were my cousin Brigitte and most of her friends, a Canadian girl named Jackie, Peter Frohwein, and Schurli Chaimowitz, a Viennese Jew. My life became normal. I felt at home in Bogotá with my friends and my new family.

Chapter 5
BOGOTÁ: THE TEENAGE YEARS

Even though we spent a lot of time together, my relationship with friends was superficial. We usually went out as a group to the movies or just to walk around. Parties were our main activity. We got together at Schurli's house and played World War II records, mostly big band music, and we danced. We were fascinated by American music and listened to Tommy Dorsey or Glenn Miller for hours, with the girls or without them. I had a strange relationship with Jackie, the Canadian girl, who lived two blocks away. She really liked Meinhard, another guy in our group, but in the afternoon when she was alone, I often went to her house and we fooled around in her living room, which was at street level. We picked the living room so that we could look out of the window and watch for her parents. We never got completely undressed or went all the way.

Once when I planned a party at my house, my mother insisted I invite two eighteen-year-old boys, Pablo and Gerardo, whose parents were her friends. Although these guys came from German-Jewish families, they grew up in Bogotá, went to school there, and were more Latin than German. They spoke perfect Spanish in addition to German. We got along very well and became friends. Our old gang began to disintegrate when Meinhart left for the United States and Schurli returned to Vienna with his parents. Since Schurli had most of the records, that was the end of listening to big band jazz. Pablo and Gerardo were more sophisticated, more grown up and mature, but not more intellectual. Soon we were joined by Gustl (Ernesto), a Viennese guy who was quite a bit older, and Bandi, a Hungarian, and finally by Victor, the only real Colombian in our group. We formed very close bonds and were constantly together. Our group was named *La Rosca*, which means "the ring." Everybody knew us and wanted to belong to our group and to be invited to our famous parties, get-togethers, and poker games. It now comes to me as no surprise that we all enjoyed playing poker and other card games because all of our parents played cards constantly.

This group stayed together for nearly six years. We had many girls in our group, as well as other guys who came and went, but it was always the original six, including myself, who were the nucleus. We were so close that no one planned a weekend without consulting with the others. We all lived in the same neighborhood, except for Victor, the Colombian, who was an intern at a Catholic high school. After we turned eighteen, several had their own cars or the use of one, like I did. This convenience helped with our get-togethers and weekend trips to the country. We usually spoke only Spanish among ourselves, probably in deference to Victor, who did not speak German. When we played poker during the week, one or two of us drove to Victor's school and parked the car under the wall. He would climb the wall and jump onto the roof of the car. Then, at 2 or 3 AM, we would take him back. He would climb on the car again and scramble over the fence. I still don't know how he got down inside the wall on the other side without getting hurt.

My whole life was focused on our group. We told each other everything, sometimes shared girlfriends, and in good Latin American tradition visited the red-light district together. Colombian fathers used to take their sons to their favorite brothel and encourage their sons to spend time with their special prostitute to "learn the ropes." Well, we did not do that. Our fathers were too German. Colombians were still so old-fashioned that when we had parties at our homes and invited Colombian girls, they had to be chaperoned by a sister, mother, or aunt who would sit in the living room during the whole party, and, of course, take them home again. Once in a while, the girls were allowed to come with a brother, which made things much easier.

Our lives were completely carefree. We played cards at least twice a week, had parties on the weekends, and went to *tierra caliente* (hot country) down the mountains to get some heat and a change of climate. We drove in two cars and had a ball. Maybe that was what I needed then, after Shanghai, but it was an empty life. We did not read books or go to plays or concerts or do anything else that was stimulating. But I learned how to enjoy life, party, dance, drink, and shed my strict German upbringing.

On April 9, 1948, something terrible happened in Bogotá, which probably, unconsciously, helped me to decide later to leave Bogotá. Here is what I wrote in English on April 26, 1948 to my step-parents, who were by then in Monroe, Louisiana:

I am really sorry that I didn't write earlier, but we were so excited and upset during these weeks that I just couldn't. Well, the most important thing is that they didn't do anything to any of us here, and that they also didn't bust or burn our shop. I'll just tell you one thing: it's terrible, actually it was terrible, because now it is already much better. As you probably read in the papers, on the ninth of April, a day I'll never forget, somebody here killed Jorge Eliezer Gaitan, one of the most important political leaders of Colombia and a presidential candidate. It was just like the 17th of July in Shanghai, the day of the American bombing—a day of horror. You cannot imagine it. The mob here robbed and burned stores and businesses in the center of the city and many government buildings in one day and one night. Helped by armed policemen, the mob robbed every store on the main street of the city. After two days, the government finally called out the Army. Only they could overpower the mobs and *police, after much killing and a lot of shooting. The mob also opened the jail and freed 3,000 criminals. They burnt the Ministry of Justice building, where all their records were filed. The Army now took over, and put the city, as well as the country, under martial law. That means that anyone who doesn't obey the Army gets shot. They also set a curfew after 7 PM (and now 9 PM) which might last another month until they completely reorganize the Police Force here in Bogotá. If you could believe that thousands of people can plunder and burn the center of a city for two days without any resistance, you might be able to imagine how the city looks. It is unbelievable how people can ruin a city within such a sort period of time. The business center is ruined. The only thing they could not get were the banks, and that was our luck, because if they had, the country would have been bankrupt. Just imagine kids and grown-ups, masses of people armed with knives, called machetes (normally used in the jungle), roaming the streets, ready to kill anybody who gets in their way. These mobs looted liquor stores first and got drunk, and that made it even more dangerous. They announced that as soon as they have nothing else to loot in the city, they'd come to the residential neighborhoods. Luckily, that did not happen. Two or three Jewish men were killed when they tried to defend their shops, which was the silliest thing to do. Fortunately, nothing happened to our store.*

This was not a pleasant experience for an eighteen-year-old, even one who had lived in a Shanghai ghetto. But life got back to normal in a few months, and I kept living my carefree life with my family and La Rosca.

Four of us once took a trip by car to Cali, the second biggest city in Colombia. It took two days because the roads were narrow and very curvy. First we had to drive from Bogotá, which is at 8,500 feet, to Girandot, which is at sea level and very hot; then we travelled up the mountains again through Armenia and back down to Cali. The mountain roads were very dangerous with only one lane each way and no divider. If you were stuck behind a slow-moving truck and you wanted to pass it, you had to cross over into oncoming traffic without being able to see beyond the curves. This lack of visibility often caused accidents. For us it was an adventure, but otherwise, in hindsight, my life was boring. Card playing became such a bad habit that when we went into the warm climate outside of Bogotá for the weekend with the girls, we played poker until 5 AM while the girls watched. How were these girls able to tolerate such treatment?

I started to think about leaving Colombia.

Chapter 6

A LIFE IN AMERICA

The years passed quickly, and things took an unexpected turn. Our friend Victor was shot and killed, supposedly during a burglary at his house; we never found out exactly what happened. I was now about twenty years old. I had not really had a girlfriend. Ruth, the girl in our group that I liked, preferred Pablo. I tried to get her away from Pablo. For years I carried her picture in my wallet—she was my secret love. It annoyed me that Pablo did not stop going out with her, since he did not really like her. Many years later, Pablo confessed that he only went out with her so that I would not have her, because he was convinced that she was not a good person, and the wrong woman for me. We will never know.

I got bored working at our store, so I started to look for a job. I found one with a fairly large and important import company, agents for some of the largest American manufacturers, such as Quaker Oats, Eastman Kodak, etc. Later, I also worked for two movie distribution companies.

On December 17, 1951, my mother suddenly died. Even though she had many attacks, which were never explained to me, she did not seem seriously ill. It happened very fast, without a long illness. After my mother died, I started to think about leaving Colombia. I began reading the *Aufbau,* the German-Jewish weekly published in German in New York, to which my family subscribed. I started dreaming of a life in New York. I studied newspaper ads for American restaurants, stores, and the New World Club, a refugee social club. I discovered more and more reasons for leaving Colombia. The main reason was that my mother was not there. In addition, some of my good friends were marrying or going with Colombian Catholic girls. Deep inside, I knew I did not want to spend the rest of my life in Colombia, even though I had such an easy life there after the hardships of my youth in Shanghai. I felt something was missing, and I was ready to take a risk and start a new life once again.

When I told Onkel Sally that I wanted to leave for the United States, he told me that I would receive my share of my mother's inheritance. She supposedly owned fifty percent of the store. Eventually, I received only about $2,500, which seemed to me far from the actual value. Onkel Sally later married a German-Jewish woman from New York.

I wrote to my stepmother, now living with her husband in Monroe, Louisiana, asking her to help me obtain an affidavit. She did this good deed with great pleasure, with the help of a distant relative, the multimillionaire Texas owner Nieman Marcus. Mr. Marcus simply wrote a letter to the American Consulate in Bogotá, and that was enough for me to get a visa. I had to obtain a new German passport so that I would qualify for the German quota, which was very high, and never used up. I simply went to the German consulate in Bogotá, produced my birth certificate, and got my passport. My English was by then quite fluent again, since I had learned it first in Shanghai. I also had taken lessons at the Colombian-American Institute in Bogotá.

It was arranged that I would first visit Lillie and Henry in Monroe, with the understanding that it was just a visit. Then I would take a trip through the United States and later decide where I would settle. Just before I left Colombia, I received $4,000 from Germany as restitution for having lived in Shanghai, which Germany considered a "camp." This very money helped me pay for my voyage to the United States, the irresistible destination of many immigrants.

I got a dozen letters of recommendation for jobs from my parents' friends. Just before my departure, I celebrated my 24th birthday with a giant costume party at our house in Bogotá. It was the party of the year. Some of my friends had such effective costumes and masks that I did not recognize them. Half the neighborhood watched people walk into our house, and a photographer took pictures, and I still have a collection of photographs from this farewell party. It was a grand sendoff for me. I still talk about that party with my cousin Brigitte, who now lives in California, and, along with Pablo, the only one with whom I am still in touch.

I left Bogotá in July 1953. I flew again via Barranquilla to Miami for an overnight stay, and from there traveled by train to the Deep South, where I was met at the Monroe train station by Lillie and Henry. We embraced, and Lillie cried, but I felt immediately that we were not as close as in the past. After all, I was now twenty-four years old, and seven years had passed since I last saw her. Yet, I was very happy to see them again. Monroe at that time was a very small, very Southern town of about 30,000 people, with a large black population and much poverty. I could hardly understand the heavy Southern accent with which people spoke, even though my English was very good by then. The Southern drawl was like a different language to me.

Lillie and Henry lived in a small, not very elegant apartment and had just opened their own furniture and appliance store. Most of their customers were Black. They worked practically day and night to make a go of it, so I spent a considerable time with them at the store. They belonged to a small, rather tight-knit Jewish community. I was introduced around and wined and dined and showered with Southern hospitality to an extent I found overwhelming.

Lillie and Henry had arrived in Monroe from Shanghai in 1948 on an affidavit from Henry's relatives, who have lived in Monroe for about 100 years. Even though Lillie and Henry received some financial help initially, they both got jobs and had to work incredibly hard. Lillie, who was tough by nature, did not mind. Even though she was already sick then with chronic stomach problems from Shanghai, she was too proud to accept handouts. She wanted to prove to the Jewish Southerners how she could work. Lillie tried to make it as nice for me as possible. She even introduced me to two girls whose parents were among the richest Jews in northern Louisiana. My stepparents, of course, wanted me to stay in Monroe, but I absolutely hated it. It was too small, too provincial. I could not get used to the Southern way of life. I noticed that black people had to ride in the backs of buses, and that public bathrooms were segregated. I told Lillie that I would not make a decision until I had finished my trip around the country. Very reluctantly, they let me go again.

Two of my jobs in Bogotá had been in distribution of American films. I had gotten it into my head that I wanted to work in the same industry in the States. So when I arrived in Los Angeles from Monroe, I learned the distribution headquarters were in New York, which reinforced my desire to head for New York. It was great to see Gert, my best friend from Shanghai, in Chicago, where I also saw my cousin Jochem and his mother. But New York was my destination. I stopped in Cincinnati to see Lillie's sister and brother-in-law from Shanghai, and arrived with very little money in New York a month after I left Bogotá in 1953. I was met by my cousin Hans, the son of my mother's sister, whom I did not remember at all since he was sent early from Germany to England on the famous *Kindertransport* and grew up in Scotland. He eventually joined his parents in New York, but they passed away before the war was over.

Hans got me a room with a communal bathroom for $10 a week on the same floor as his own in a walk-up rooming house on the Upper West Side. Even for 1953, it was rather cheap. The primitive conditions did not bother me even though I was used to luxury in Colombia. I was also used to living under much worse conditions in Shanghai.

I decided to look for a job. Since I had many leads from my mother's friends, I started calling people. They were all very nice and said they would help, but I never heard from them again. On the other hand, most people I met talked me out of trying to get a job with the film companies because they were known to pay badly and the chances of getting ahead were very slim. The fact that I spoke Spanish was to my advantage, and my new friends in New York suggested that I look for a job in the export business.

One day I simply took matters into my own hands, went to an employment agency, and applied for a job in export. They gave me a slip of paper with the name of an export company, N.A. Kerson Co. Inc., located at 120 Wall Street. I arrived for an interview, and immediately got a job with a starting salary of $55 a week, which was average for 1953. Soon after that, I moved out of the rooming house. I rented a furnished room with kitchen privileges with some distant relatives, which was much more pleasant, and certainly homier. I soon became friends with the two other guys who were also renting rooms in the apartment, and that is how I got settled. Without much soul-searching, I decided to stay in New York.

And thus began the next phase in my life, which turned out to be the most stable, happy, and successful one.

I started dating as soon as I arrived in New York, and I met Erica on a blind date in 1954. I wanted to get married right away, but she was still attending Barnard College. On June 24, 1956, after Erica finished social work school at Columbia University, we were married. The party at Tavern on the Green was beautiful and emotional. I was so grateful that both Lillie and Henry, and Onkel Sally and his new wife Betty were able to attend. My one regret was that Sally and Betty walked me down the aisle. In retrospect, I wish that it had been Sally and Lillie, because they had both been married to my original parents.

In 1957, I started my own export business in New York. Erica was extremely helpful. She gave me good advice and kept me from taking risks. Beginning with half an office and working extremely hard, I was soon able to build a flourishing business, with 30 employees at its peak, exporting millions of dollars in auto parts.

My son Leslie was born on May 6, 1964. Erica had had trouble conceiving, but Leslie was worth waiting for. When I saw him in the hospital, I was flooded with good feelings. It was also the day I gave up smoking for good.

Chapter 7
RETURN TO THE PLACES OF MY YOUTH

In 1976, my son Leslie turned twelve. I decided I wanted to show him and share with him the three most important parts of my life before I lived in America. I felt like twelve was old enough for him to understand. Our first trip was to Colombia on one of my many business trips there. We went to Bogotá, the capital, and then to Medellin, the second biggest city.

Bogotá is approximately 10,000 feet high and surrounded by mountains called the Andes. At the time we visited, Bogotá had a population of about 3 million. We had lived in a neighborhood called Teusaquillo, about fifteen minutes from the center of town. I showed Leslie the whole city and the house we had lived in, which we compared to a picture I had of our house, with my mother, stepfather Sally, and our dog standing in front. We went up Montserrate by cable, which is right next to the Bull Ring and gives a spectacular view of the city. We also went to the famous Gold Museum, and we travelled outside of Bogotá and saw the underground Salt Cathedral, made entirely out of salt, so you could touch the walls and taste it.

We flew to Medellin, which is one hour by jet from Bogotá. Medellin is in a valley completely surrounded by mountains. At that time, the airport was in the middle of the city, and to land there the plane nearly touched the mountains. It came so close that we could see the cows grazing. It is a beautiful city with perfect weather, and an industrial city with many industries. My customer belonged to a country club where we spent an afternoon and even played tennis.

In 1980, when my son was sixteen, we took our second trip, to Shanghai. It was the trip of a lifetime. Not only did I want to show him where and how I lived in Shanghai in the ghetto for seven years during the war, but I organized a trip for us halfway around the world.

At the time, only group travel to China was permitted. The Chinese students who worked as tourist guides did not want us to visit Hongkew. It was a poor, working-class neighborhood, just as it had been in our day; it was not meant for tourist excursions. After a brief negotiation, we received permission to visit and be accompanied by a student guide. So we took a taxi to Hongkew. The student simply could not believe that 18,000 German and Austrian refugees had lived there during the Second World War. "We will ask a few older people," I suggested, "and then you will hear what they have to say!"

We had barely arrived in Hongkew when two elderly Chinese men confirmed just that fact, to the young man's shock. The old man used the Chinese word "Yutaning" when referring to the Jews. We visited three locations where I lived and in the last one an old Chinese lady insisted that she remembered me. Who knows if that was so, or if she was just being nice.

My trip with Leslie to Gumbinnen was probably the most emotional and the most indelible of the three autobiographical trips we took together, and I remember it in detail. In early July 1992, a few years after the Berlin Wall came down, and with it, communism in East Germany, I sat in our room in the very luxurious Hotel

Kempinsky in Berlin with my son Leslie. It was the third leg of our journey to the past.

We enjoyed a most delightful breakfast, served on sterling silver and costing $65.00. Wow! I loved every minute of the great experience I shared with my son. In our room we felt as if we were in a palace, thanks to our four-poster bed with down bedding, beautiful paintings, and a great bathroom with heated towels. We both loved Berlin; unfortunately we could only spend one night there. It is the only city where the Germans didn't ask me immediately what country I came from.

The next day, we checked out of the hotel and took a taxi to the railroad station two hours before the train departure, unaware that the station was only five minutes from the hotel. I was always very punctual, actually very early. Leslie was annoyed that we had to wait so long. The taxi driver was annoyed at the short ride, telling us in Berliner slang that he had lost his place in line. Our train left from track 12. It was a special train (*Sonderzug*) for the tour to East Prussia. I was disturbed by the word *Sonderzug* because it reminded me of the special trains the Nazis used to ship Jews to concentration camps.

This tour was especially organized for Germans living in West Germany who wanted to visit their former birthplaces in East Prussia from which they had been expelled by Russia in 1945. None of these people had seen their native land in about forty years. After World War II, East Prussia was divided between Poland and the Soviet Union. The Russian part, where I come from, was practically sealed off during the Communist era—it was designated a "military zone." When the Russians defeated the Germans, they occupied East Prussia, then captured and destroyed the German military and forced out the German civilian population and made it a Russian province. Russian civilians were brought in and still live there. No Germans live there, and no one speaks German. All the streets have Russian names, as do the cities. Koenigsberg, the old capital of East Prussia and still the main city, is now called Kaliningrad. My hometown, Gumbinnen, can be found on the map as Gusev.

I had mixed feelings finding myself on that train with two hundred Germans. Those of my generation or older were born in East Prussia and were now going back to re-live their pasts and show their birthplaces to their children and grandchildren, just as

I was doing. The big difference was that Leslie and I were probably the only two Jews on that train.

I had heard about these special trips through a German woman, a diplomat who worked at the German consulate in New York. The trip began by train from Berlin via Warsaw to Grodno. There, special buses crossed Lithuanian territory, then drove back into Russia. First stop was Gumbinnen, then Koenigsberg, and finally Danzig (now Gdansk, Poland), after which they returned to Berlin.

After a long wait, we boarded the train. Our first-class compartment with beds was small, but we even had a little sink. Everything was spotless on this German train. It is a relief after the night train we had taken a few days earlier from St. Petersburg to Moscow. The Russian train was also first class, but the difference was incredible—its toilet smelled so bad it was barely usable.

Then the train started to move. Everybody stood in the corridor to look out the windows, so we joined them. Only German was spoken. There were a lot of families, mostly couples of my age or older, with their grown kids. Everybody was in a good mood because they were going to see their former homeland again. I was much more apprehensive, not knowing what to expect or what I would find in Gumbinnen, especially since I remembered little about it. All I had was the name of the street of our house and store and a little map my cousin made me, plus a very old photograph of the buildings.

Some of our fellow passengers started talking to us in German. I answered in German, saying my son spoke only English. This piqued their curiosity.

"Where do you both live?" they asked me in German.

"In New York," I said.

"And where are you going in East Prussia?" they asked me.

"Gumbinnen," I said, "that is where I was born."

Then they asked, "And when did you leave Germany?"

"Just before World War II," I said. "In July 1939, to be exact."

That opened their eyes. They now knew we were Jewish. Soon a crowd gathered around us, and we were treated like celebrities, as if German travelers had never seen Jews before. Everybody wanted to talk to us, and many spoke English to my son. I had very mixed feelings speaking to Germans my own age, because they are usually defensive, falling back on tired excuses, like "I was on the Russian front," or "I was an American prisoner of war," and "I really did not know what was going on in Germany."

Younger Germans in their 20s and 30s were more genuine and pleasant. They seemed to have no guilt. Conversations in the corridor went on until we finally went to sleep at midnight. We woke up a little later as the train came to a stop. It was Warsaw, the capital of Poland. No one got off or on; it was just a border check. Leslie and I kept track of every country we visited in our many travels, so we decided it was legitimate to add Poland to the list because we actually stopped there. Before we went back to sleep, we reserved two spaces in the dining car for breakfast at 8:00 AM.

The next morning, we were seated at big tables with other Germans and the same kind of conversations started again. By now, practically everyone spoke English to us for Leslie's benefit. We were lectured about Germany's past, and about the history of East Prussia. We befriended a few German couples whom we saw many more times during our trip.

When we reached Grodno we were told to transfer to modern long-distance buses for the five-hour trip to Gumbinnen after lunch. Lunch was an uncomfortable experience. We all had to wait in the parking lot of a rather large building in the broiling sun, until we were let into the restaurant in groups of about forty. Then, to compound the unpleasant experience, the service was terrible, the food inedible, and the heat over 90 degrees F, without air conditioning.

After lunch, we were milling around in the parking lot again waiting for the new buses, when suddenly, we heard a commotion and saw a man stretched out on the pavement. Before long, an ambulance came and took him away. Later we learned he was from our group and had had a heat stroke. Our whole group waited an hour and a half for the new modern buses, but they never appeared. Finally, the tour provided us old school buses with very uncomfortable seats. The man who collapsed was back from the hospital and was with us again. In spite of the long delay, heat, and the lack of air conditioning, spirits were high.

We traveled on a beautiful one-lane highway with large trees on either side, whose branches sometimes touched us above. It seemed as if we were driving through a tunnel of trees. Back into Russia (former East Prussia) from Lithuania as we approached Gumbinnen, some of the people recognized certain landmarks. We passed lush rolling hills. I had never learned the East Prussian hymn, nor many other German folk songs, traveling songs, nor, of course, the marches. Amazingly, however, I remembered some of the tunes. I am sure a number of my older friends back home would have shivered had they heard the singing of this Nazi-like music as it grew louder and louder, but it did not bother me. I suspect a lot of men had their little bottles of Schnapps with them, and were happily imbibing.

As we entered Gumbinnen, I pressed my face to the window. I saw no cars, only buses and trucks. There were hardly any people on the streets. It was about 8:30 PM, but there was still daylight, since East Prussia is far enough north to benefit from sunset around 10:30 PM in the summer. Our bus and the ones behind us stopped in the very center of town. Leslie and I got off with our bags and were given a loud farewell by our fellow passengers, most of whom went on to Koenigsberg. A "Volga German" from the tour company who spoke a little German met us. [Volga Germans are Germans who settled in Russia during the reign of Catherine the Great. A German herself, she invited thousands of them to live in Russia. During World War II, they were sent to Siberia. After the war, some returned to the Russian section of East Prussia, their original homeland.] He took us to the hotel, located next door, and, after negotiating in Russian with the Russian woman concierge at the desk, told us that there were no more rooms available, but not to worry. We could stay in his room. Then he proceeded to take us up the stairs to a room which was much more dilapidated than any I have ever seen in a hotel anywhere in the world: used towels on the table, unmade beds, open pipes in the bathroom, used drinking glasses, and dirty dishes. I urged Leslie to leave our stuff in our room so we could go out and try to find our house before dark. I met another Volga German hanging around in front of the hotel trying to make some money as a guide. He spoke some German and had an old German street map on which we found the exact spot on the corner of Koonig's Strasse and Hindenburg Strasse, where I had lived. I became very excited about seeing again the house in which I was born. It did not occur to me until later that this was the town in which I would still be living if it weren't for Hitler.

When the guide finally said, "Your house must be right at this corner where we are standing now," I quickly took out my old photograph of the house. We crossed the street, and it was my original home. It had the same archways as in the picture, the same number of windows. Across the street from the river Pissa, just as I was told. Leslie started taking pictures of the house. I was overcome with emotion, and I thought of my father. Soon, a crowd gathered to see what these foreigners were doing. The Russian residents of our house looked out of the windows where laundry was hanging to dry. They shouted down in Russian to ask if we were going to buy the house. The grand arched entryway, now bricked shut, was replaced by two separate entrances. The house had been subdivided into quarters for many families. In our day, only two families lived there.

Our guide and the Russians entered into a running conversation. We were asked if we wanted to go inside, but I said no, I wouldn't remember anything about the interior anyway. We stood in front of the house for two hours, staring, and in my case, trying to remember. Seeing the house in which I was born, and my home for my first six years was a moving experience.

Back at our hotel, we went to dinner. Crowds of German tourists from a different group were in the hotel's little bar, singing and carrying on. We were unable to approach the bar, which sold only vodka and Russian beer, so we entered the dining room, which seemed fairly clean, and sat down at a table. The food dished out to us was barely edible. We picked at the food and ate a lot of black bread with butter. We each had an imported Coke. The water was undrinkable, and the bottled water had a medicinal aftertaste. As we finished eating, we noticed people at other tables eating what looked like ice cream on a stick. Leslie said, "Finally something edible. After all, what can they do to ice cream?" We ordered ice cream, and when the waitress brought it, we simultaneously took a big bite. No luck. It did not taste like ice cream. The German guests were eating and drinking with gusto and laughter.

Our guide said our hotel was formerly the Kaiser Wilhelm Hotel. It was the only good hotel in Gumbinnen. My cousin later told me that our fathers used to go there every day for coffee and cake. How different it must have looked then! Our store, which had been in the family since 1880, used to be right next to our house. It was probably destroyed or bombed during the fighting in Gumbinnen. In its place, the Russians built a five-story apartment building which was already decaying. The condition of the postwar construction throughout Russia is far worse than the pre-war German construction or even the pre-war Russian construction. The old houses and buildings in Gumbinnen, like my former house, still looked solid even though many had not been kept up and were badly in need of painting.

After a very long day, we were exhausted. We went to bed in our clothes because we felt so uncomfortable there. We slept well, tired from the long train and bus ride and the excitement of being in Gumbinnen. We got up early the next day, had a breakfast of black bread and coffee, then met our tour guide again for a tour of the city. Before we started out, I reconfirmed the taxi that would later take us to Vilna. I was assured it would arrive at noon. All our arrangements in Russia involved negotiations, with people screaming and gesturing. And there was always a crowd watching us.

When I asked our guide where the taxi for our city tour was, he laughed. "Oh, no taxi, we walk—there is not much to see; this is a small town." So we walked for about one hour while he pointed out the highlights like the old cemetery, which had a section for German Jews who lived in Gumbinnen before the war. I now regret that we did not enter the cemetery, because both of my grandparents died in Gumbinnen before the war, and were probably buried there. We saw the house where Werner von Braun, the famous rocket scientist, was born, and the school my cousin attended.

We passed many barrack-like buildings now inhabited by Russian troops. Gumbinnen was always an army town. When I asked our guide why there were no stores, he answered, "no one has any money to buy anything." Most people worked in the two factories in town or in the fields in the countryside. Our shoes were covered with dust from walking, since the sidewalks were not really paved. On the way back to the hotel, he showed us some newer government buildings, but the tour was generally disappointing. We did see the landmark of Gumbinnen, the famous statue called *Elchstandbild* (elk statue), which now stands in a small park on the old

Konigsstrasse and no longer on Magasinplatz across from the hotel Kaiserhof, where it had stood before the war.

As we walked along the River Pissa, we saw teenagers holding hands. I guess there is romance even in Gumbinnen. When I asked our guide where these kids got their nice jeans, he said, "Oh, these jeans are from Poland, where they are so much more advanced."

We waited for our taxi to take us to Vilna. The guide had promised us the best and newest car they had, so we wouldn't get stuck on the road. When the car finally appeared, it was a Russian model, but clean and new. The driver did not speak English or German, so it was impossible to communicate with him. He had only one eye, and he smiled continuously.

We had to overcome one more potentially dangerous problem: we had only a Russian visa, but just before we left on our trip, Lithuania had become an independent country. No one was able to tell us if we needed a visa for Lithuania or if the Russian visa would do. I had called the Lithuanian consulate in Berlin, and they said they did not really know. Russian authorities did not know either. I explained it to our driver in Russian, who told us (through the guide) not to worry; he would take care of everything at the Russian/Lithuanian border. So we piled into the taxi for the four-hour ride. I figured we would get to Vilna by 4 PM with plenty of time to spare.

We had booked a flight back to London via Zurich. Our flight out on Swissair was only at 7 PM. But I always worry about unforeseen problems. Our drive was through the beautiful countryside, with big old linden trees along one-lane highways. It occurred to me that our name, Lindenstraus, must have come from linden trees.

When we arrived at the border town, I began to get nervous. The driver asked for our American passports as our car stood on the line on the Russian side of the border. The driver crossed a bridge to the Lithuanian side, and again there was a long line. Somehow our driver managed to get nearly to the front of the line where Lithuanian soldiers stood guard. When our turn came, he motioned for us to stay in the car. He got out and showed our American passports. Two very young soldiers, not more than 17 years old, with machine guns, looked at us in the car, smiled, and to our great relief, let us pass.

So we arrived in Vilna on schedule. The capital is over one thousand years old and crumbling within. The airport, which looked nothing like an airport, was just an old house with policemen stationed in front. When we got out, we noticed handwritten bulletins with flight numbers and departure times posted on a wall of the house. The Swissair office was on the second floor. Once in the office, I felt like I was in a different world. It was modern, bright, cheerful, and air-conditioned. After I obtained our tickets, we went to the restaurant, a huge room with many empty tables, and waitresses sitting around them. The menu was four pages long, in Lithuanian and German. But for whatever we ordered, the answer was *nyet*, not available. "*Nyet, nyet*, and *nyet*." Finally they brought us some meat, which wasn't bad at all. The waitresses again sat down at the next table to watch TV with us while we were eating. Since we had plenty of time, I talked to a few policemen at the airport. As soon as they found out we were Americans, they only wanted to talk about basketball. They knew every player on the Knicks. Later I discovered that Lithuania was a power in basketball with a great national team.

We finally got on the plane, which taxied to the runway using the same highway on which we arrived by car. I had never seen anything like that.

The trip lasted six days, but we only stayed three days because Leslie needed to return to work in the States. We had already been to Moscow and St. Petersburg and spent a day in London just to see one day of tennis at Wimbledon.

Chapter 8

MY LIFE NOW

This was my journey, and it was quite an adventurous one. I have lived on four continents. First was Germany, specifically my boyhood home, Gumbinnen. Second was Shanghai, to which we fled to escape the Nazis, and where my formative teen years were spent. Third was Bogotá, Colombia, where I lived with my birth mother for seven years, and where I slowly matured into a young man with ambition.

Now I live on the Upper East Side, a few blocks from my son, his wife, and their two children, my grandchildren, Jessica and Aaron. Jessica is seventeen, and

Aaron is fifteen. Wow, life has changed, but I am so glad it did! I am so grateful to have my grandchildren in my life, and to be able to see them regularly. I grew up without grandparents and mostly without parents, and I find my role as a grandfather to be satisfying and miraculous.

A year after Erica died, Margie came into my life. She is terrific, and we enjoy each other's company. We travel, and she keeps me going. Often she comments on how very German I seem, even though I left Germany when I was ten!

Many people have asked me to talk about how I felt growing up in Germany and Shanghai, and what it was like to revisit these places as an adult. The truth is, I don't have any feelings about it. I have plenty of feelings about good things—I could write volumes about my wonderful grandchildren, how it felt to present my father's *tallis* (from 1906!) to Aaron at his bar mitzvah, and how it felt to attend Jessica's high school graduation, but it is much harder to talk about my past. Perhaps I learned to suppress my feelings. It isn't easy to grow up with divorced parents, to have to flee your native country, to live in a ghetto and be subjected to tropical diseases, to lose both your parents. Perhaps this is why I can remember my childhood with such detail and clarity—I suppressed my feelings so I could cope. My son Leslie said in an email,

By separating emotions from the memories, you could clearly recall details of what you did, but not how you felt. While this may seem empty, unfortunate, or even sad, I think it must have helped you get through life without carrying the emotional baggage that could have been a huge negative and prevented you from being happy, optimistic and successful (which you have been and still are!)

As for my trips with Leslie, perhaps I did not feel particularly emotional about visiting Colombia because I lived a more or less normal life there. I certainly felt emotional in Germany when I found my original house. Shanghai, I don't remember what I felt, but Leslie does. He wrote:

I had lots of feelings when we visited Shanghai. I was 16 and tried to imagine myself as your age living there, under those conditions, playing in the poor peoples'

lanes with Gary. I wondered where was his house relative to yours? As we searched for your street, I was exhausted by the heat and yet driven by the possibility of finding it. And then, yes, we found the street! I vividly remember the moment we saw your house with the number still on it. And when, through the translator, the old Chinese woman came out and told us that she remembered there was a boy who lived in her house many years earlier, it sent chills down my spine! I visualized the stories you had told me. The open out-house on the roof; the bad food, the illnesses, the crowded rooms divided only by a hanging carpet. Could I have survived under those circumstances and conditions? No, I was not tough enough. I thought of Grandma Lillie ruling the house and trying to take care of you, although by age 16 you probably did not listen to her. I thought of Uncle Isi and where did he have his dental practice. I wondered about your job and your adventures and the dangers and close calls that happened (some of which you may not have been aware of). I wondered where was the check-point with Goya? I wondered where did people die. And, strangely, I don't think I asked you any of these questions at the time, or shared any of my thoughts and feelings.

I enjoy telling my story at the 92nd Street Y or the Witness Theater or to whomever wants to hear it. I feel like it is my duty to educate people about the Jews of Shanghai during World War II. I am grateful to have had the life I had, which was not a conventional one, but I know I was loved, first by my parents, and then by my step-parents. I am fortunate to have had wonderful friends and a successful business and to have found Erica, to whom I was married for fifty years. I take immense pleasure in Leslie's family. I am grateful to Margie. I play tennis, I stay well, and I pray every day. I continue to try to do good in the world. And I always tell my two grandchildren, "if I didn't end up in Shanghai I would not be here today and neither would you..."

Appendix

Gumbinnen - Königstraße m. Kriegerdenkmal

Our store around 1900, to the left our house , below our store in 1937

Lindenstraus, Gumbinnen

GEGRÜNDET 1883

Großhandlung in Kurz-, Weiß-, Wollwaren, Trikotagen, Konfektion, Baumwoll-
waren, Damen- und Herren-Wäsche, Putz, Spielwaren und Sport-Artikel

BANK-KONTO:
e Bank, Depositenkasse Gumbinnen
eck-Konto: Königsberg i. Pr. 10656
Fernruf Nr. 2126

GUMBINNEN, den

Letterhead of the store, picture of my grandparents

Geburtsurkunde.

~~Nur gültig in Angelegenheiten der Kranken-, Unfall-, Invaliditäts- oder Altersversicherung.~~

Vor= und Zuname *Louis Lindenstraus*

Geburts=Tag und Ort *21ten Juni 1893, Gumbinnen*

Vor= und Zuname, sowie Stand des Vaters *Jacob Linden-*

straus, Kaufmann;

Vor= und Zuname der Mutter *Cäcilie geb. Friedmann*

Gumbinnen, den *25 ten März* 18*00*.

Der Standesbeamte.

(Siegel.)

My father's birth certificate. My mother Lilly (left) with her sisters Herta and Irma

Geburtsurkunde.

Nr. 205.

Gumbinnen , am 29. Juni 19 29.

Vor dem unterzeichneten Standesbeamten erschien heute, der Persönlichkeit nach

de kann,

der Kaufmann, Louis Lindenstrauß ,

wohnhaft in Gumbinnen, Bismarckstraße 55,

und zeigte an, daß von der
Liesbeth Lindenstrauß,geborenen Olschewitz, **seiner**
Ehefrau ,

wohnhaft bei ihm, dem Anzeigenden,

zu Gumbinnen in seiner Wohnung ,
am achtundzwanzigs ten Juni des Jahres
tausend neunhundert neunundwanzig, vor mittags
um drei Uhr ein Knabe
geboren worden sei und daß das Kind den Vornamen
Gerd
erhalten habe.

Vorgelesen, genehmigt und unterschrieben.
Louis Lindenstrauß .

Der Standesbeamte.

R u d a t .

Daß vorstehender Auszug mit dem Geburts-Haupt-Register des Standesamts

zu Gumbinnen

gleichlautend ist, wird hiermit bestätigt.

Gumbinnen, am 11. Juni 19 38.

Der Standesbeamte.
In Vertretung.

My birth certificate

With my father 1932

With my mother on the balcony of our house

With my mother in Cranz, a resort near Koenigsberg

Verzeichnis über das Vermögen von Juden

nach dem Stand vom 27. April 1938

des **Lindenstraus, Louis,**   **Kaufmann**

in **Danzig,**   **Breitgasse** ~~xxxxxx~~ 121/2
                                       bei Hermann.

Angaben zur Person

Ich bin geboren am **21. Juni 1893.**

Ich bin Jude ... der Ersten Verordnung zum Reichsbürgergesetz vom 14. November 1935, Reichsgesetzbl. I S. 1333)

und ~~deutscher~~ ... Staatsangehöriger

Da ich — Jude deutscher Staatsangehörigkeit ... bin, habe ich in dem nachstehenden Vermögensverzeichnis **mein gesamtes inländisches und ausländisches** Vermögen angegeben und bewertet.

Da ich Jude fremder Staatsangehörigkeit bin, habe ich in dem nachstehenden Vermögensverzeichnis mein inländisches Vermögen angegeben und bewertet.

Ich bin ~~xxxxxxxx~~**geschieden seit 14.8.1936.** geb. _____

~~Mein Ehegatte ist der Rasse nach jüdisch / nichtjüdisch~~ und gehört der _____ Religionsgemeinschaft an.

Angaben über das Vermögen

I. Land= und forstwirtschaftliches Vermögen

Lage des eigenen oder gepachteten Betriebs und seine Größe	Art des eigenen oder gepachteten Betriebes	...	Wert des Betriebs ℛℳ	...

II. Grundvermögen (Grund und Boden, Gebäude)

Lage des Grundstücks	Art des Grundstücks	Wert des Grundstücks ℛℳ	...
Gumbinnen/Ostpr.Königstr.1	**Geschäftsgrundstück**	**116,600.**	**1/3**
dito, Hindenburgstr.4.	**Geschäfts=u.Wohngrdst.**	**46,000.**	**1/3**

Vermögensverzeichnis ...

Certified a true + correct copy

Louis D. Smith

LOUIS D. SMITH
Notary Public, Ouachita Parish, Louisiana

My father's net worth, as required by the Nazis in 1938

My stepmother Lilly in Koenigsberg 1938

NORDDEUTSCHER LLOYD
BREMEN

SCHNELLDAMPFER
»SCHARNHORST«

AM 10. JULI 1939 VON BREMEN

über Rotterdam—Southampton—Palma de Mallorca—
Barcelona—Genua—Port Said—Suez
nach Colombo, Singapore, Manila, Hongkong, Shanghai,
Yokohama, Kobe

Schedule of the German luxury ship Scharnhorst sailing from Bremen to Shanghai with
partial passenger list.

NORDDEUTSCHER LLOYD BREMEN

Frau Margot
Lindenstrauss
Gerd Lindenstrauss
Herr Heinrich
Lindenstrauss
Frau Anna Lindenstrauss
Herr Joachim
Lindenstrauss

PASSAGIER
LISTE

NORD
LLOYD

**Schnelldampfer ›Scharnhorst‹
am 10. Juli 1939 ab Bremen**

Herr Louis Lindenstrauss

7

C o p y !

Certificateof Death.

Nr.10 -/1940   Shanghai Febr.23 rd. 1940

Before the undersigned official appeared today, according to her

passport, the German subject, Marg_ot Sara L i n d e n s t r a u s,

no profession residing at Shanghai and declared as follows: The

German subject Louis Israel L i n d e n s t r a u s, born June

21 st, 1893 at Gumbinnen, profession merchant, last place of

residence, Shanghai, had died on Dec. 21 st.,1939 at 2, 15 p.m. at
the Emigrant's Hospital , Washing Road, Shanghai.

This record has been read to the announcer, agreed upon and signed

personally as follows: Marg ot Sara L i n d e n s t r a u s .

Closed.

The Consulate Secretary I Class, commissioned to represent the

German Consul General, S t a r k .

Remark:

        Marriage: Koenigsberg Nr. 433/391/1939

                Issued.

        Shanghai, Febr. 27 th., 1940

The German Consul General,
by order
signed: E r a u e n r a t h .

official seal.

A 8196/47

This translation has been compared
with the German original and found
correct.
  Shanghai, March 28th, 1947

JUEDS HE GEM NDE
COMMUNAL ASS CIATON OF
CENTRAL EUROPEAN JEWS
LEGAL DEPARTMENT

Dr. Otto Kertschonel

Sterbeurkunde des Vaters in Schanghai

My father´s death certificate dated December 21 1939 in Shanghai

77

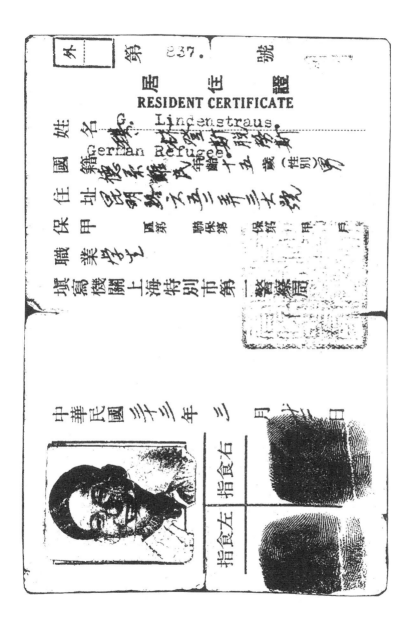

居　任　證

RESIDENT CERTIFICATE

姓　名　G. Lindenstraus.

國　籍　German Refugee.

My residence certificate

Kadoorie school in Shanghai, class picture. I am on the upper right

Shanghai Boy Scouts, troop 13 in Shanghai. Gary bottom left and I am on top left

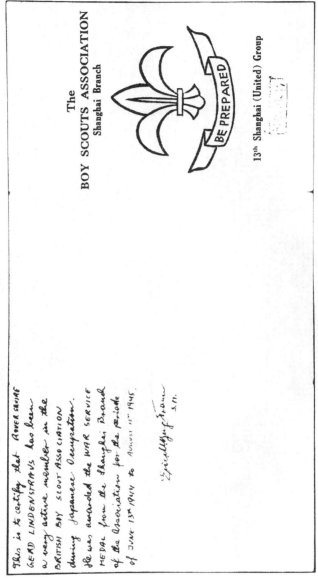

My Boy Scout Certificate

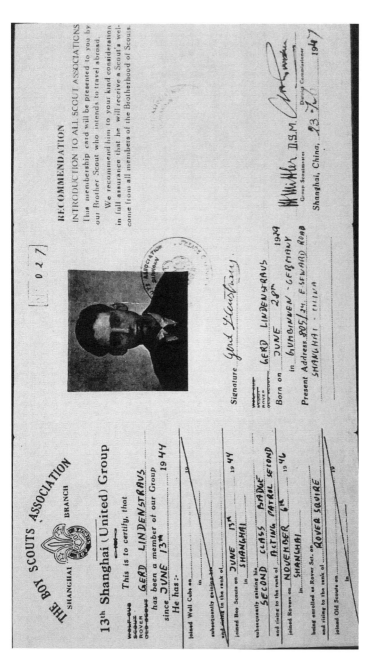

My Boy Scout Certificate

Chanukah greetings from an American Jewish soldier to all of us kids included one American dollar

HEADQUARTERS
UNITED STATES FORCES
CHINA THEATER
RECRUITING SECTION

5th. January 1946

To Whom it May Concern.

    Gerd Lindenstraus has been in my employ since the 6th.
of November 1945 as Office Boy,and has proved himself
competant in the following tasks.
    His typing is 35 to 40 words per minute with accuracy.
    He is fully capable of maintaining a filing system.
    He can,efficiently and concientiously perform the
duties of a messenger,and can be trusted with any materiel
of a confidential nature.
    In short I have found this young man,willing,capable,
concientious and absoutely trustworthy,and will unhesitatingly
recommend him for any job embodying his past experience or
for any job demanding learning ability.

sincerely

Gilbert A.Campbell
S/Sgt. Ordnance Dept.
Recruiting Sargeant.

Recommendation letter Page

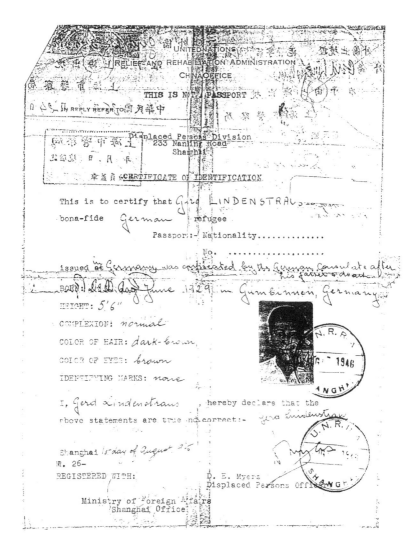

My travel document

HEADQUARTERS CHINA SERVICE COMMAND
Office of the Adjutant General

Shanghai, China
30 September 1946

TO WHOM IT MAY CONCERN.

      This is to certify that Mr. Gerd Lindenstraus
has been employed with the Adjutant General's Personnel
Section from 10 January 1946 until present date as a
clerk.

      During this period his services have been per-
formed in a very satisfactory manner. He has proved to
be a diligent, honest and very efficient employee. I recommend him to anyone desiring the services of a capable
and efficient worker.

JOHN J. SMITH
Major   AGD
Asst Adj. Gen

Another recommendation letter

上 海 市 警 察 局
SHANGHAI POLICE BUREAU
HEADQUARTERS

REF. NO. 2014,
185 FOOCHOW ROAD
SHANGHAI
DATE 19/2/1947,

For the Columbia Consulate,
San Francisco, U.S.A.

This is to certify that the police records of
the undermentioned person has been checked to
contain nothing detrimental to his character.

Name   Age Nationality   Date of arrival

LINDENSTRAUSS Gert 17 German Refugee   Aug. 1939.

Commissioner,

Shanghai Police Bureau.

Good conduct certificate, and my farewell picture with Gary 1947

Goodbye photo with Lilly and Henry

In San Francisco with friend Alex on the way to Bogota

In Bogota with girlfriend Ruth

With Vera Salomon at a masquerade party at my house

With first cousin Brigitte

With friend Meinhart on our roof and our famous friendship group "La Rosca" with Victor, Gerardo, Bandi, Pablo and Rodolfo and I, back in the midth.

In front of our house in Bogotá with my mother and her husband Sally

My wedding to Erica and her mother Anka in New York 1956

The house in Gumbinnen, where I was born, picture taken by Leslie
in 1992

My son´s wedding to Michelle in New York 1996

My granddaughters graduation from High School in June 2017 with her brother
Aaron and Michelle and Leslie

During World War II, German, Austrian and Polish Jews fleeing the Nazis found refuge in Shanghai, China. By 1941, Shanghai's Jewish community numbered nearly 20,000. This unlikely spot became a haven for Jews largely because it was the only place in the world they could enter without a visa. In recent months, the Museum of Jewish Heritage has endeavored to collect materials that illuminate the unique story of Jewish refugees in Shanghai.

Former Shanghailander Gerald Lindenstraus, who recorded a video testimony at the Museum in 1992 and who has donated his own family documents and photographs to the Museum's collections, has been working closely with the research staff to develop a body of exhibitable material relating to the Shanghai refuge. Several months ago, Museum Director Dr. David Altshuler and Mr. Lindenstraus sent an appeal to former Shanghailanders throughout the world, many of whom Mr. Lindenstraus knew from his youth. In response to

the mailing, the Museum's collection of Shanghai material has burgeoned to include many significant artifacts, documents, and photographs that reflect the diverse aspects of Jewish life in Shanghai. Among these newly acquired objects are passes that Jewish residents carried with them in order to leave the ghetto, identification cards, and Jewish newspapers published in Shanghai.

The Museum continues to collect artifacts and photographs from the Shanghai refuge as well as memoirs and reference books on this subject for our research library. If you are interested in making a donation, please contact Esther Brumberg, Research Coordinator, at 212-687-9141.

The Museum's research staff also is interested in obtaining any information on the dentist, Dr. Walter Schindler. Born in Berlin in 1890, Dr. Schindler emigrated from Germany to Shanghai in 1939 with his wife Gertrud Weisenberg Schindler and daughter Ellen Ursula, and subsequently immigrated to the United States in approximately 1946 or 1947. A large collection of material relating to this family was donated to the Museum, and we ask that any Shanghailanders who have information on the Schindlers please contact Ms. Brumberg.

Museum of Jewish Heritage

A LIVING MEMORIAL TO THE HOLOCAUST · 1998 ANNUAL REPORT

Some of the English books in Prof. Wiehn's edition on Shoah & Judaica / Jewish Studies

Rebekka Wedell and George Wedell, **The Samuel Meyer of Hanover Connection**
1st Edition 2017. 206 pages. € 24.90. ISBN 978-3-86628-560-6

David Guttmann, **Homecoming.** Jewish life and suffering in Hungary and on the 'Exodus' to
Palestine back via Hamburg and Bergen-Belsen to Eretz Israel. 1944–1948
2015, 144 pages. € 18,00. ISBN 978-3-86628-534-7

Jacques Stroumsa, **Violinist in Auschwitz.** From Salonica to Jerusalem 1913–1967.
1996, 110 pages, photos, € 10,12. . ISBN 3-89191-869-0

Jerzy Czarnecki, **My Life as an "Aryan". From Velyki Mosty through Zhovkva to
Stralsund.** 2007, 173 pages, many photos, € 14.80 €. ISBN **978-3-89649-998-1**

Zwi Helmut Steinitz, **As a boy through the hell of the Holocaust** – From Poznań through
the Kraków Ghetto, Płaszów, Auschwitz, Buchenwald, Berlin-Haselhorst, Sachsenhausen, to
Schwerin and over Lübeck, Neustadt, Bergen-Belsen and Antwerp to Eretz Israel 1927-1946.
2009. 396 pages, € 24.80. ISBN 3-86628-250-8; 978-3-86628-250-6

Max Kaufmann; **Churbn Lettland:** The Destruction of the Jews of Latvia Foreword by
George Schwab. Preface by Paul A. Shapiro. Introduced by Gertrude Schneider
Translated from the German by Laimdota Mazzarins. Edited by Gertrude Schneider and
Erhard Roy Wiehn. 2010; 296 pages. € 24,00. ISBN 978-3-86628-315-2

Konrad Goerg, **We Are What We Remember.** Germans, Two Generations after Auschwitz
Voices to Remind Us. In Remembrance of Erwin Katz. Forewords by Horst Eberhard Richter
and by Erhard Roy Wiehn 1st Edition 2010, 116 pages. € 9.95. ISBN 978-3-86628-342-8 1st

Israel Aharon Ben Yosef, **Judaism as a Festive Way of Life.** A Rabbi´s Reflections on
Jewish Holidays. Translated from German by Ute Ben Yosef. Edited by Erhard Roy Wiehn
First Edition 2012. 68 pages, € 14,80. ISBN 978-3-86628-442-5

Association for Researching the History of the Jews in Blankenese, Erhard Roy Wiehn (Edts.)
Cherries on the Elbe. The Jewish Children's Home in Blankenese 1946-1948. Translated by
Judy Grossman. 2013; 230 pages, € 14,80. ISBN 978-3-86628-428-9

Hans-Hermann Seiffert, **"My Beloved Children!"** Letters of Hella Schwarzhaupt to Her
Children from Internment in Camps Gurs and Récébédou. 1st Edition 2015. 128 pages, many
photos and documents. € 15,30. ISBN 978-3-86628-521-7

Erhard Roy Wiehn, **Jews in Thessaloniki.** translated into English by James Stuart Brice.
2004, 74 pages 12,-- €. ISBN 3-89649-909-2

Bookorders in your bookstore or www.amazon.com or directly

Hartung-Gorre Publishing House
D-78465 Konstanz / Germany
eMail: verlag@hartung-gorre.de
http://www.hartung-gorre.de